Comments on other *Amazing Stories* from readers & reviewers

"*Tightly written volumes filled with lots of wit and humour about famous and infamous Canadians.*"
Eric Shackleton, *The Globe and Mail*

"*The heightened sense of drama and intrigue, combined with a good dose of human interest is what sets* Amazing Stories *apart.*"
Pamela Klaffke, *Calgary Herald*

"*This is popular history as it should be... For this price, buy two and give one to a friend.*"
Terry Cook, a reader from Ottawa, on *Rebel Women*

"*Glasner creates the moment of the explosion itself in graphic detail...she builds detail upon gruesome detail to create a convincingly authentic picture.*"
Peggy McKinnon, *The Sunday Herald,* on **The Halifax Explosion**

"*It was wonderful...I found I could not put it down. I was sorry when it was completed.*"
Dorothy F. from Manitoba on **Marie-Anne Lagimodière**

"*Stories are rich in description, and bristle with a clever, stylish realness.*"
Mark Weber, *Central Alberta Advisor,* on **Ghost Town Stories II**

"*A compelling read. Bertin...has selected only the most intriguing tales, which she narrates with a wealth of detail.*"
Joyce Glasner, *New Brunswick Reader,* on **Strange Events**

"*The resulting book is one readers will want to share with all the women in their lives.*"
Lynn Martel, *Rocky Mountain Outlook,* on **Women Explorers**

THE MAD TRAPPER

AMAZING STORIES

THE MAD TRAPPER

The Incredible Tale of a
Famous Canadian Manhunt

HISTORY/CRIME

by Hélèna Katz

PUBLISHED BY ALTITUDE PUBLISHING CANADA LTD.
1500 Railway Avenue, Canmore, Alberta T1W 1P6
www.altitudepublishing.com
1-800-957-6888

Extreme care has been taken to ensure that all information presented in
this book is accurate and up to date. Neither the author nor the
publisher can be held responsible for any errors.

Publisher	Stephen Hutchings
Associate Publisher	Kara Turner
Series Editor	Jill Foran
Digital photo colouring and maps	Scott Manktelow

We acknowledge the financial support of the Government
of Canada through the Book Publishing Industry Development
Program (BPIDP) for our publishing activities.

Altitude GreenTree Program
Altitude Publishing will plant twice as many trees as were used
in the manufacturing of this product.

We acknowledge the support of the Canada Council for the Arts which
in 2003 invested $21.7 million in writing and publishing throughout Canada.

Canada Council   Conseil des Arts
for the Arts   du Canada

National Library of Canada Cataloguing in Publication Data

Katz, Héléna, 1964-
The mad trapper / Héléna Katz.

(Amazing stories)
Includes bibliographical references.
ISBN 1-55153-787-7

1. Johnson, Albert, d. 1932. 2. Police murders--Rat River Region (Yukon and
N.W.T.). 3. Criminals--Rat River Region (Yukon and N.W.T.)--Biography.
I. Title. II. Series: Amazing stories (Canmore, Alta.)

FC4172.1.J6K38 2004   364.152'3'097191   C2004-902707-7

An application for the trademark for Amazing Stories™
has been made and the registered trademark is pending.

Printed and bound in Canada by Friesens
2 4 6 8 9 7 5 3 1

To the men who joined the manhunt,
and to their families, who waited for their safe return.

Contents

Prologue

Albert Johnson crouched inside the trench in his cabin, clutching a gun in each hand. He could hear the men outside, firing at him and trying to bash in his door as they raced past. Listening carefully, he realized he was far outnumbered; this time they had come with a much larger group. It was essential for his own safety that he keep them from storming his refuge.

He knew their bullets couldn't penetrate the double rows of thick logs that surrounded the bottom of his cabin, but they could splinter the door and window. Taking advantage of a lull in the action, he stood up and stuck the barrel of one of his guns right up against a loophole he had made in between the logs. Then he began to fire. He would be fine as long as he could keep the police at bay. The longer he kept on shooting at them, the more likely they would tire and go away. He wasn't scared of his intruders. With their guns, flares, and sticks of useless dynamite that wouldn't even light, the men were annoying him more than anything.

Suddenly, an explosion crashed through the silence of the stalemate. Johnson dove into the safety of his trench as his cabin began crumbling around him. The door disintegrated, the roof blew off, and one of the walls caved in towards him.

He gripped his weapons and prepared for the police's next attack.

Chapter 1
Stranger in Town

lbert Johnson carefully placed the metre-high stick upright beside the other one and wedged it into the sand on the river-bank. Then he straightened up and stepped back a few paces. Aware that other people were watching, he fixed his piercing blue eyes on the target, gripped a pistol in each hand, and shot the top off each stick. Then he crossed his arms in front of himself and shot again. He repeated this display of marksmanship a few times, shaving an inch off each stick every time. It didn't take long for word of his proficiency with weapons to spread around the community.

At about 5 feet 9 inches and 175 pounds, Johnson wasn't a big man, but he had a sturdy build and his stooped shoulders looked like they had carried many a heavy pack. About 35 to 40 years old, he was a quiet, taciturn loner. He didn't want anyone prying into his business, and it certainly wouldn't hurt to let people know he was a good shot.

Johnson had recently arrived in the sleepy settlement of Fort McPherson, located in the northwest corner of the Northwest Territories, just north of the Arctic Circle on the east bank of the Peel River (upstream from where the Peel and the Mackenzie Rivers meet). His arrival on July 9, 1931, had generated a certain amount of attention due to the unconventional form of transportation he had been using. Most men travelled the area's waterways in birchbark canoes, but Johnson had built himself a crude raft consisting of three large logs. Since he didn't have much in the way of possessions, he had figured this slapdash vessel would meet his needs and get him to where he wanted to go.

As it turned out, the raft held together, but it took him off course. About 50 kilometres upstream from Fort McPherson, he saw several Native men standing on the shore. "Is this the Porcupine River?" he shouted to them.

"No," they yelled back. "It's the Peel River."

The headwaters of the Peel and Porcupine Rivers are a few kilometres apart in the Yukon. While the Peel flows into the Northwest Territories, the Porcupine heads into Alaska. Johnson cursed as he continued floating down towards the settlement. He had taken a wrong turn somewhere along the way and wasn't in the northern Yukon at all. Somehow, he had crossed over into the Northwest Territories.

Johnson pulled up onshore just five kilometres from Fort McPherson, abandoned his raft, and walked the rest of the way to the settlement to buy supplies. Meanwhile, the men who had seen him floating by on his raft had returned to the settlement and told others about his presence. People were surprised to hear that he had been negotiating the northern rivers in such a crude raft. Curious, they watched the stranger wander through the community. They noticed that he had very little equipment for surviving in the North. They also noticed that this wouldn't be much of a problem for long — Johnson seemed to be carrying an unusually large amount of money. Their curiosity grew. Who was this man? Where did he come from, and where did he get all that cash?

In the 1930s, the community of Fort McPherson consisted of little more than a few wooden buildings. The Hudson's Bay Company (HBC) had established a trading post there in the 1840s, and Northern Traders Limited had soon followed suit. The area was rich in furs, and trapping and fishing were at the heart of the Northern Native peoples' livelihood. Once the trading posts had been established, these peoples began trapping even more extensively.

Each June, towards the end of the month, the Gwich'in would travel to Fort McPherson to trade furs and buy supplies. The first two weeks of their visit were spent selling furs, paying off debts, and buying goods for the coming year. Since it was one of the only times of year when everyone in the area left their camps out on the land and came together in one place, it was also an opportunity to spend time reconnecting with family and friends.

This exciting and busy time was marked by the Dominion Day (July 1) festivities, which included foot races, canoe races, and football games. It was also during these long sunny days that the steamboat made its yearly visit, loaded with flour, sugar, and tea. The Gwich'in happily snapped up most of these supplies during their annual shopping spree.

It was in the midst of this pleasant, celebratory atmosphere that Albert Johnson arrived at Fort McPherson. But while others around him were socializing and having a good time, it was clear that Johnson just wanted to load up on supplies and be on his way. He wasn't much of a talker and responded gruffly — to the point of rudeness — to even the friendliest of advances.

Johnson set up camp just upstream from Fort McPherson, about a kilometre and a half from the settlement. He stayed there for a few weeks while he got organized for the next leg of his trip. During that time, he made it quite clear that he wasn't interested in entertaining visitors at his tent. On one occasion, three Native men who went over to shake his hand, as was the custom, were rebuffed. On another occasion, a storm blew into Fort McPherson. It was the kind of weather that sent everyone scurrying for shelter. When a small group of men walked over to Johnson's tent and asked him if he would like to join them at the trading post to wait out the storm, Johnson refused their hospitality. Instead, he closed up his tent and burrowed inside alone.

This kind of behaviour was deemed very unusual. While the Arctic tended to attract individualists, the area's difficult terrain and unforgiving elements meant that people were nonetheless dependent on each other. Civility was important because people needed to know they could rely on their neighbours if the need arose.

But the newcomer had other things on his mind. Soon after he arrived at Fort McPherson he bought a 16-gauge Iver Johnson single-barrel shotgun and a box of shells from Bill Douglas at Northern Traders Ltd., paying cash for his purchase. He also picked up food and plenty of ammunition both there and at the HBC trading post. During his short stay near the community, Johnson purchased enough food and supplies to get him through the coming winter. On one particular day, he arrived early at the HBC post. When the store opened, he went inside and bought $700 worth of supplies.

The shopkeepers in Fort McPherson noticed that Johnson had a rather peculiar habit of buying an item with a $20 bill (a large amount of money in those days), and pocketing the change. Then he would wander up and down the aisles, pick out another item, and pay for it with another $20 bill taken from a different pocket. Each item was purchased separately. Despite this oddity, the shopkeepers said he was a good customer. He knew what he wanted, bought it, and then went on his way. He wasn't interested in chatting or exchanging pleasantries with the trading post employees and seemed particularly reluctant to answer any questions about himself. Indeed, he only spoke whenever he needed to order supplies.

The trappers at the trading posts continued to wonder about this quiet stranger who had arrived on a crudely made raft with few supplies and lots of cash. And they weren't the only ones. During his annual visit to the settlement, Anglican Bishop W.A. Geddes heard about Johnson's presence in the community and made a mental note of it. When he returned to Aklavik, the administrative centre for the Mackenzie Delta region, he reported Johnson to Inspector Alexander Neville Eames, the commander of the Western Arctic subdivision of the Royal Canadian Mounted Police (RCMP).

At that time, the Great Depression had swept across the continent and a number of men were leaving their homes and farms in search of a better life. Good fur prices and gold prospecting were bringing them to the Canadian North in hopes of improving their fortunes. But many of these desperate men were not prepared for the rugged terrain of the North or the harsh Arctic weather that prevailed for much of the year.

Winters, which ran from late September to mid May, were long and cold at this latitude north of the Arctic Circle, with average temperatures of –25 degrees Celsius. December through to February was the harshest time, with temperatures averaging –32° C and sometimes dropping even lower. Winds from the northwest could get as high as 65 to 80 kilometres per hour. In addition, in a region with few roads, dog teams were an essential form of transportation in winter. Mushing wasn't a skill that southerners necessarily possessed.

Given that so many ill-prepared men were venturing north, the RCMP had made it a routine practice to interview strangers in town as a safety precaution. Authorities wanted to make sure these men were physically fit and adequately prepared to spend the winter in the isolation of the Arctic wilderness. Not only could inexperienced men put themselves at risk, they could also endanger the lives of RCMP members or anyone else who might be required to come to their rescue when they got themselves into trouble. The interviews saved these men from their own incompetence in the High Arctic.

After speaking with Bishop Geddes, Inspector Eames asked Constable Edgar Millen to go check on Johnson. Millen had joined the RCMP in 1920 after attending military school and moving to Alberta with his parents. He had volunteered to serve in the North, and had been posted to Aklavik three years later. In the summer of 1931, the 30-year-old Belfast-born Mountie had been sent to head up the two-man detachment in Arctic Red River. Now known as Tsiigehtchic, the detachment was 80 kilometres east of Fort McPherson and 110 kilometres south of Aklavik. The Mounties had to patrol large areas, and the RCMP members at Arctic Red River were also responsible for covering Fort McPherson since the community didn't have a detachment of its own at that time.

It was shortly after Millen arrived at Arctic Red River that he received the order from Eames to interview Johnson.

Millen headed out on July 20 and arrived in Fort McPherson the next day. After asking a few people around the settlement about Johnson, he learned that the mysterious stranger had floated down the Peel River on a curious-looking raft. One of the traders also mentioned that Johnson had spent a fair bit of money buying equipment. Armed with this limited information, Millen went looking for Johnson to ask him a few questions and establish whether or not he could take care of himself in the North.

Johnson was buying more supplies when Millen caught up with him. Not in a mood to talk, the mysterious man said little in response to the Mountie's questions. He told Millen that his full name was Albert Johnson, and that he wanted nothing to do with the police because there was always trouble whenever they were around. Johnson then lied about where he had been. He claimed that he'd spent the previous winter in the Prairies and had come into the North by heading down the Mackenzie River.

Millen was well aware, however, that Johnson had floated down the Peel River from the direction of the Yukon. Millen made a mental note of the lie but decided not to press the issue. When asked where he would be spending the winter, Johnson told Millen he planned to head west along the Rat River, and would likely continue on through the Richardson Mountains and over to the Yukon. He was vague about his

Constable Edgar Millen

plans, and it was clear to Millen that Johnson wanted to be left alone.

In addition to policing, the RCMP's duties in the North at that time included taking censuses in their district, routinely checking in on trappers and prospectors (particularly during the long and lonely months of winter), and issuing trapping licences to non-Natives. Millen informed Johnson that he needed a trapping licence if he planned to trap in the area. The officer told the strange man that he could buy the licence from the Arctic Red River or Aklavik RCMP detachments or save himself the trip by purchasing it from Millen himself immediately. Johnson didn't express any interest in following up. Millen thought the stranger with the slight Scandinavian accent was odd, but figured that perhaps it was the result of spending too much time in the bush.

To the employees of both of the trading posts in Fort McPherson, it was evident that Johnson wasn't planning to live in the settlement. His purchases indicated that he was gathering enough supplies together to leave town, but he needed a means of transportation to do that. In late July, Johnson bought a 12-foot canoe from a Gwich'in man who lived across from his camp. He then loaded up his gear and paddled away down the Peel River.

A few days later, Johnson realized he was lost. Knowing that there was no one around to ask for directions, he figured his best bet was to backtrack to a small trading post that he'd passed on his way out of Fort McPherson. Johnson paddled skilfully against the current and pulled his canoe up onto the shore at the mouth of the Husky River. He then stepped out to ask Arthur Blake, an ex-RCMP officer and the owner of the small trading post along the Husky, for directions to the Rat River. Johnson explained to Blake that he was he heading to the Yukon and that he had somehow missed the spot where the Husky intersects with the Rat.

Before Blake could even offer up directions, Johnson demonstrated that he had some knowledge of the area. He pointed out the small creek behind the trading post and indicated that he believed he could reach the Rat River by navigating along the creek and making a number of short portages with his canoe. Blake knew the area well and was sceptical — it sounded like a difficult route. He told Johnson that it would be easier to go back along the Peel River and follow the south branch of the Husky River to the Rat. But Johnson, who seemed to have an unshakeable confidence in his wilderness skills, had already made up his mind. That afternoon, he climbed back into his heavy canoe and headed up the creek behind Blake's home. He made his way through a chain of lakes and portages and soon reached the Rat River.

A few kilometres above the mouth of the river, Johnson was forced to navigate through a section of treacherous white water. During the Klondike Gold Rush, gold miners had nick-named this section of the river "Destruction City." It marked the beginning of a series of difficult rapids that eventually headed up towards McDougall Pass. The riverbed rose 360 metres in the span of 56 kilometres. Large boats couldn't navigate these waters, so gold seekers had been forced to cut their vessels down to a more manageable size. The banks were littered with abandoned supplies and the remnants of boats that had been chopped down by their owners or destroyed by the rapids. In the winter of 1898–99, some 50 to 100 prospectors had waited along the banks of Destruction

City for the weather to break long enough for them to continue their trek in search of fortune. Four men had died of scurvy before the spring had arrived.

Johnson, however, did not meet with a similar fate at Destruction City. Indeed, it was a testament to his strength and skills that he was able to negotiate the dangerous rapids in his heavy canoe. Despite his success, he decided to take a break in his journey and stay in the Northwest Territories for the winter. It was late in the season and Johnson was concerned that he would not have enough time to travel to the Yukon, find a place to live, and build a cabin before winter set in. He stopped about 19 kilometres up the Rat River — some 65 kilometres north of Fort McPherson — and picked an isolated spot on which to build a cabin. As police reports later indicated, he chose a promontory that was surrounded by the Rat River on three sides.

Johnson built a small cabin that was about 8 feet by 12 feet, using logs that were around 12 inches in diameter. The structure was about 5 feet high at the front and 4 feet in the back. The door was only 19 inches wide. The roof was covered with two-foot thick frozen sod. A tiny window beside the door allowed him to look out on the clearing in front of his house. The outside of the cabin was reinforced, particularly along the bottom, with extra logs to keep out the cold. Sod in the cracks between the logs froze like concrete during the winter.

Once the cabin was built, Johnson stored some of his

supplies inside his new home and put the rest in a cache outside. The cache, which consisted of a platform suspended in the trees, would keep at least some of his food out of harm's way in case the cabin was ever destroyed by fire. When all of his supplies were suitably stored, Johnson settled in. He used a tin can stove for heating and cooking.

In the sparsely inhabited areas of the Arctic, it wasn't unusual for people to stop in whenever they happened to be passing by someone's cabin. Visiting helped to break up the isolation and loneliness of an Arctic trek and gave travellers a chance to warm up in the dead of winter. But whenever wandering northerners would knock at Johnson's door, he refused to let them inside his cabin. It was said he even slammed his tiny door in their faces. Visitors were an unwelcome intrusion. And, while most northerners respected independence, word of his unsociable behaviour spread through the area like a cold northern wind. People began to grow suspicious of Johnson.

Chapter 2
Trouble on the Trapline

inter comes early in the Far North; snow often starts to fall as soon as September. The temperature drops, blizzards swirl, and winds begin to howl. The nights become longer and the waking hours are blanketed in darkness. The weak sun shines only a few hours each day. It is at this time of year that the silence and isolation across the barren Arctic region seems to be most acute. Canoes are put away until the spring. Snowshoes and dog teams become the main means of transportation as rivers freeze and harden enough to turn the summer's waterways into the winter's roads. Men and their teams must be careful not to break through rotten ice. They must also take care not to get wet. At temperatures of –40

degrees Celsius, frostbite and hypothermia can set in quickly.

In late summer 1931, Albert Johnson had set up his cabin near the traplines of three Native men: William Vittrekwa, William Nerysoo, and Jacob Drymeat. The Rat River area had been Native trapping territory for centuries. Trappers did not need to register their traplines back then, but non-Natives had to get a licence to trap. People owned their own traplines and others respected them.

As William Nerysoo followed his trapline in the area of the Rat River in December 1931, he realized that someone had been tampering with his traps. And his weren't the only ones to have been messed with. Other Native trappers also found their traps lifted, torn up, or hung on trees, and their bait scattered. This was very upsetting, as these men relied on trapping to feed and clothe their families. They sold the furs of their quarry at the trading posts each year to buy supplies. Their lives and livelihoods depended on their traplines. Who could be sabotaging them?

Johnson was a newcomer to the district — and an unfriendly one at that. The men suspected immediately that he was the culprit, but they didn't dare confront the strange white man who lived alone and shunned the company of others. He had threatened the people in the area with his rifle and they were scared of him. The three Native trappers wondered whether Johnson was trying to send them a message by tampering with their traps, but they weren't about to walk up to his door to ask.

Instead, William Nerysoo decided to turn to the RCMP for help. He made the 110-kilometre trek to the RCMP's Arctic Red River detachment at the junction of the Arctic Red and Mackenzie Rivers. On Christmas Day, Nerysoo told Constable Millen that a strange white man had been springing his traps and hanging them on trees. Nerysoo said he believed the man's name was Albert Johnson and explained that Johnson lived alone in a cabin about 24 kilometres up the Rat River.

Constable Millen ordered Constable Alfred King and Special Constable Joseph Bernard to take a dog team to Johnson's cabin to see whether he had a trapping licence and to investigate whether Nerysoo's charges were true. Neither Millen nor King anticipated any trouble — this all seemed like a rather routine call.

Twenty-five-year-old Constable King had joined the RCMP in 1926. A year later, after having volunteered to serve in the North, he had been posted to Dawson City, where he'd stayed for two years. He had then gone back down south for about a year before heading north again, to Aklavik, in 1930. At one time, King had been responsible for the nine-ton RCMP schooner *Kingston*, which travelled between Aklavik and Herschel Island. He hadn't been at the Arctic Red River detachment for very long, and it was just happenstance that he'd been posted there at all. Constable Ronald Melville, who worked with Millen, had cut his foot and had gone to Aklavik to get patched up. Until he was healed, a replacement would be needed. King had been reassigned and had arrived at the Arctic Red River detachment just before Christmas to work with Millen. The two men had a quiet Christmas and then got back to work to follow up on Nerysoo's complaints.

Given the difficult terrain, the harsh winter climate, and the predominantly Native population who spoke their own languages, the RCMP in the Northwest Territories and the Yukon often hired local Natives to help their officers. These special constables were hired as guides and interpreters. They were also contracted to teach the Mounties survival skills and how to drive dog teams. Often, the special constables would accompany the Mounties on patrols. Special Constable Bernard hadn't been with the RCMP for very long. He'd joined on August 1, 1930, and had performed general duties around the detachment.

At 7 a.m. on December 26, 1931, Constable King and Special Constable Bernard set off in the early morning darkness. It was a bitterly cold, two-day trip to Johnson's cabin. The two men hitched up a couple of dog teams, comprised of two to five dogs each, and headed out. After travelling west for nearly 50 kilometres, they spent the night in Fort McPherson with Hudson's Bay trader John Firth. The next morning they headed down the Peel River. After travelling another 40 kilometres, they stopped at the mouth of the Rat River and set up camp beneath the stars. It was a nippy –34° C. The exhausted pair tied up their dog teams, built a fire, burrowed inside their sleeping bags, and went to sleep.

They rose early the next morning and trekked the last 24 kilometres to Johnson's cabin, arriving there at 10 a.m. on December 28 — just as the sun was beginning to rise.

Smoke was drifting out of the chimney of the cabin, and Johnson's crude homemade snowshoes — made of bent willow frames — were resting against the outside wall when the men arrived. They knew Johnson was either inside the cabin or nearby. Constable King could tell that Special Constable Bernard was terrified, but he had no idea why. Perhaps Bernard had heard things about Johnson from other Native people in the area. From his cabin, Johnson had a view on three sides. There was three feet of snow in front of the cabin and thick willow brush and spruce behind it.

The two constables left their dog teams by the riverbank and headed towards the cabin. King snowshoed to the little front door and pounded on it. Shouting so that his voice could be heard inside and out, he announced that he was a member of the RCMP. He tried to get Johnson to open the door to talk with him, but there was no response from inside. King stood out in the open as he explained that the detachment had received complaints that someone was interfering with traplines in the area, adding that he wanted to ask Johnson a few questions about it. Again there was no response, just an eerie silence.

Inside the cabin, Johnson lifted a burlap sack that was covering the tiny 12-inch window to the right of the door. He peered out at the police officer who was trying to get his attention. King could see that Johnson was doing something with his hands. "I saw Johnson looking out through the cellophane window," King later recounted. "I thought he was dressing. But I know now he must have been getting his gun ready. I realized later he was loading his gun."

When he spotted King looking back at him, Johnson immediately covered the window again. Once again speaking loud enough to be heard inside the cabin, the officer reiterated the reason for his visit. He still got no response. After waiting for about an hour, King realized that Johnson had no intention of opening the door to answer any questions. The Mountie, like the locals before him, found this behaviour odd. It was unusual for people in the North to ignore a knock at the door. They usually invited visitors in for tea, or at the very least, offered up some sort of greeting.

Constable King knew he couldn't force his way into the cabin without reinforcements and a search warrant. Because he didn't have a radio (radios were not standard policing equipment in the early 1930s), the constable had no way to reach anyone to tell them that Johnson was being unresponsive to the police's inquiry. King realized he would have to go to the detachment in Aklavik to report Johnson's behaviour. The commanding officer in Aklavik, Inspector Eames, was also a justice of the peace and would have the authority to issue the warrant. The larger detachment also had more men, who could then return to the cabin with King to deliver the warrant.

It was a 130-kilometre trip from Johnson's cabin to Aklavik, and it would take Constable King and Special Constable Bernard two days of travel by dog team to get there, and two more days to get back. But they had little choice; if Johnson was up to something, the matter would have to be dealt with.

Chapter 3
Officer Down

klavik, which means "Place of the barren land grizzly bear" in the language of the Inuvialuit, was the administrative head-quarters for many government services for the Western Arctic. It was a thriving community of about 400 people. An Anglican mission had opened up there in 1919 — about seven years after the Hudson's Bay Company had set up a trading post. The RCMP then established a detachment there in 1922, and the All Saints Anglican Hospital was built in 1926 under the guidance of Anglican Bishop Geddes. The hospital could accommodate up to 50 patients.

RCMP Inspector Eames, who had just turned 48 on Boxing Day, headed up the Aklavik detachment of nine men.

Eames had joined the RCMP in 1913 and within seven years had been promoted to corporal, sergeant, and then inspector. He became the commander of the Western Arctic subdivision in June 1929. The Welsh-born Mountie had remained loyal to the force during World War I, turning down an opportunity to be quartermaster sergeant of the 131st Battalion overseas. The superintendent of the RCMP's "E" division at the time had described Eames as being "one of the smartest non-commissioned officers under my command."

Aside from their general policing duties, Eames and the other RCMP officers at Aklavik were responsible for cutting and hauling wood, hunting, fishing, and cooking for themselves. They kept an eye on the people in the district, checking cabins during patrols to make sure residents were fine. Whenever there were medical emergencies, it was the Mounties who went out to rescue people and bring them to the hospital in town. Despite the additional work, these tasks gave the RCMP the opportunity to get to know everyone in their district.

On December 29, 1931, Constable King and Special Constable Bernard arrived in Aklavik and told Inspector Eames about their attempt to meet with Albert Johnson. Eames, too, found Johnson's behaviour suspicious and issued a search warrant. Concerned about possible trouble, he also ordered Constable Robert McDowell and Special Constable Lazarus Sittichinli to accompany King and Bernard back to Johnson's cabin.

Before they left, Eames wanted to make sure that all four men were well armed. He instructed them to put rifles in their sleds in addition to carrying their side arms. Besides being there to back up King, McDowell would also be able to help bring Johnson into Aklavik if they were able to capture him.

The four men left Aklavik at 7 a.m. on December 30 with two dog teams. After camping overnight along the trail, they arrived at Johnson's cabin the next morning at about 10:30. They had travelled speedily from Aklavik and were hoping to deal with the Johnson matter quickly so that they could celebrate New Year's Eve at a party being hosted by a Hudson's Bay trader in Fort McPherson — it promised to be quite the event.

The group agreed that Constable McDowell and the two special constables would stay back while Constable King took the lead. As McDowell took cover with a rifle below the steep riverbank 18 metres away, King crossed the clearing and walked up to Johnson's cabin. He picked up an axe that he found there. "I intended to knock down the door if he didn't answer," King later explained.

Because he was already suspicious of Johnson's behaviour, King didn't stand directly in front of the door. Nor did he leave himself vulnerable by standing near the cabin's window. Instead, he leaned his back against the wall of the cabin and stretched his arm towards the door, knocking twice with the back of his left hand. "Are you there Mr. Johnson?" he called out. Johnson's snowshoes by the cabin and the smoke coming from the chimney suggested that he was. King then informed Johnson that the RCMP had come with a search warrant this time and that they would be forced to break down the door if he didn't open up.

Without warning, Johnson fired his gun at King from inside the cabin, the bullet ripping through the closed door. King felt a burning sensation as the bullet tore into his chest. Then he crumpled to the snowy ground.

The men below the riverbank were stunned. McDowell watched in shock as his partner fell to the ground. With King lying by the front door of Johnson's cabin, the wounded constable was an easy target for follow-up shots. McDowell knew that he had to distract Johnson or else King would soon be dead. He grabbed his Lee Enfield rifle from his sled and fired at the cabin in hopes of diverting Johnson's attention away from King. The plan worked. Johnson fired at McDowell twice through a loophole he had made in between the logs in his cabin. The second bullet narrowly missed the Mountie.

McDowell's fire gave King a cover and bought him a bit of time. The injured officer managed to crawl off to the side and away from the cabin. He used the shelter of some nearby bushes to keep away from the gunfight. Then, in terrible pain, he stood up and circled towards his partner while keeping out of Johnson's line of fire. He staggered over to McDowell and slid down the riverbank.

McDowell looked at King's wound and realized it was serious — he would have to act quickly in order to save King's life. It was –42 degrees Celsius and McDowell needed to get the wounded officer to the hospital in Aklavik before he froze to death. He figured there was no point in trying to storm Johnson's cabin because it was doubtful that he and the special constables would be able to get Johnson out without reinforcements. Besides, the intense cold could bring on shock and put King in even greater danger if he waited.

The men had just travelled nearly 28 hours from Aklavik, and the dogs were tired from having run the last 50 kilometres that morning. Still, McDowell knew he had no choice: the group would have to speed back to Aklavik to save King's life. McDowell dumped the supplies from his sled to make room for his partner. Then he and the special constables put King on the sled, wrapped him in furs to try to keep him warm, and strapped him in. At about 11 a.m., less than half an hour after they had arrived at Johnson's cabin, the men left for the return trip to Aklavik. McDowell was an excellent musher who, a year earlier, had conducted routine mail runs between Aklavik and Baillie Island, a distance of almost 100 kilometres. But this run was different. A life was at stake.

Though he was just 23 years old at the time, Constable McDowell was no stranger to medical emergencies. A quiet fellow from St. Vital, Manitoba, he had been a Mountie for four years. He'd enlisted in the RCMP in 1927 and had quickly earned a reputation as a first-class musher. One year he had gone out on a 173-kilometre patrol to rescue an old trapper who had seriously injured his right eye and was in terrible pain. The man had been in agony for more than two weeks and was virtually helpless. McDowell had applied heat to the eye to relieve the pain and had brought him to the Anglican Mission Hospital in Aklavik. The trapper had been contemplating suicide when McDowell had arrived and rescued him. Now the quiet Mountie was mushing to save King's life.

With the wind chill, it was about –67° C. Frostbite was more than likely at that temperature, so the men kept an eye on King's face to make sure it was fine. In addition to dealing with the bone-chilling cold and the fatigue of the dogs, the group also had to break a new trail because a fierce wind had already erased their tracks. During parts of the journey back to Aklavik, the two special constables would follow McDowell. At other times, they would run ahead to make a trail for the increasingly tired dogs.

Most of the journey was made in darkness. Since the trail wasn't completely straight and the ground was uneven, on a few occasions the men had to carefully lift the sled with their wounded comrade on it and then just as carefully place it back down again. King lay on his back in the sled, stoically enduring the continual burning sensation and soreness from his wound while struggling to breathe in the cold air. He could hear the almost continuous crunch, crunch, crunch of McDowell's mukluks as he prodded the dogs to keep going.

The men travelled through a blinding blizzard, harsh temperatures, and howling winds as they covered about

Officer Down*

130 kilometres in a record 20 hours. They made only two brief
stops during the journey to make some tea, and arrived at the
Anglican Mission Hospital with King in tow at 8 a.m. on New
Year's Day. McDowell had sprained a tendon in his right knee
while bringing King into Aklavik, and one of the sled dogs
had died of exhaustion out on the trail.

Acting Assistant Surgeon Dr. J.A. Urquhart examined
King and found the extent of the damage caused by the slug,
which was believed to have come from a .38 automatic. The
Mountie had avoided being mortally wounded because he
had been bending over when he'd knocked on Johnson's
door. The bullet had entered King's left side and had then
gone out his right. It broke two of his ribs on the way in and
two on the way out, but missed his heart by an inch.

The medical care King received, coupled with his own
excellent physical condition, allowed him to recover quickly.
Three weeks after being shot, the Mountie was up and getting
around. Nevertheless, after the shooting, Albert Johnson was
wanted on an additional charge. He had wounded an RCMP
officer — a serious offence. What had started out as a routine
police inquiry had escalated into an attempt on a police officer's life. For the RCMP, it had suddenly become much more
urgent to capture him.

41

Chapter 4
Siege

oneliness, isolation, and the darkness that shrouds the North in winter sometimes do strange things to people, making them behave in seemingly irrational ways. Northerners refer to this as "going bush." Johnson had been behaving strangely since he'd first arrived in Fort McPherson on July 9, and initially, his unfriendliness had done little more than raise a few eyebrows.

Now it was evident that he was trying hard to avoid the police. He was even prepared to shoot at them if necessary. The Mounties were puzzled by Johnson's behaviour. What had he been up to before they first went to see him at his cabin? Nobody knew. The only thing that was certain was his mistrust of the authorities. But where had it come from? Did Johnson have something to hide or was he, quite simply, going bush?

On January 1, 1932, Inspector Eames sent a telegram to his commanding officer in Edmonton to tell him that King had been wounded. The information was relayed to RCMP Commissioner J. H. MacBrien. News of Constable King's shooting appeared in Canadian newspapers about a week after it happened. Articles described Johnson, whose name was not mentioned, as a "crazed trapper." But was he really demented?

Inspector Eames knew he needed to apprehend Johnson quickly, but he wouldn't be able to leave the detachment for a few days. For one thing, the dog teams needed to rest. For another, Eames needed to assemble a bigger posse to go after Johnson since there would have to be enough men to surround the cabin. Johnson was obviously armed and it was likely that he would not surrender quickly and easily. This meant the posse would either have to wait him out in hopes that he would eventually give himself up or else storm the cabin. Either way, Eames would need a lot of men, dogs, and supplies.

The inspector wasn't sure he had enough men under his command to carry out this police operation. He had a corporal, six constables, and a special constable at Aklavik, plus Millen and another special constable at Arctic Red River. But he couldn't possibly use all of his men to bring Albert

Johnson in; some of them would be needed to carry out routine duties as well as other police matters. He certainly couldn't leave people in the district without the services of the RCMP.

As he began gathering supplies, Eames turned to the Canadian Army's Royal Canadian Corps of Signals in Aklavik for help. The corps had set up a radio station in the community in 1925 to enable communication with the outside world. Northerners referred to the government radio service as "The Voice of the Northern Lights." A source of entertainment during long winter nights, it could also be used to relay valuable information.

Eames asked the staff at the radio station — "UZK"— to send out a message to the HBC trading post at Fort McPherson. The message was to tell Native guide Charlie Rat to meet the newly formed posse at the mouth of the Rat River. A second message went out to Constable Millen at the Arctic Red River detachment asking him to meet the posse at the same place. Millen was the only RCMP officer who had actually ever spoken to Johnson. (The fugitive would not utter a word during the entire manhunt.)

Despite the difficult and windy weather conditions that dogged the North at that time of year, trappers from the district also stepped forward and volunteered to join the Mounties in their quest to capture Johnson.

On January 3, a few days after McDowell had made his 20-hour trek to save King's life, Inspector Eames set off with a posse of eight men plus one guide to make the 130-kilome-tre trek to Johnson's cabin. His men included Constable McDowell, Special Constables Lazarus Sittichinli and Joe Bernard, and civilian volunteers and trappers Ernest Sutherland, Karl Gardlund, and Knut Lang (who would later sit on the Northwest Territorial Council). Dog teams, com-prised of a total of 42 dogs, transported the men and carried the supplies, which included food for both the men and the dogs.

The posse began battling especially bad weather just after leaving Aklavik. Winds from the Beaufort Sea blew across the landscape and their fierceness stung any exposed flesh. The blowing snow created a white curtain that cut down visibility considerably. The men couldn't see more than a few feet ahead of them as they made their way around mov-ing snowdrifts. Nevertheless, they plodded along towards Johnson's cabin, moving forward as though half-blind from the snow's fury, prodding the sled dogs to keep going. They were determined to arrest the man who had shot King.

Millen and Charlie Rat met the posse two days later at Arthur Blake's trading post on the Husky River. It was the same spot where Johnson had stopped the previous summer to ask for directions. Now the posse was following in his tracks. They replenished their supply of dog food at Blake's store.

Keeping in mind that Johnson probably wouldn't sur-render easily, Inspector Eames also picked up 20 pounds of dynamite at Blake's trading post. He figured it could be used to blow a hole in Johnson's cabin if he refused to come out.

The next morning, the posse set off towards Johnson's cabin in temperatures that frequently dipped to –42 degrees Celsius. The size of the group required the sleds to be heavily laden with supplies. This extra weight, along with the extreme weather conditions, slowed the posse down significantly.

That night they camped near the spot where the Rat and Longstick Rivers meet, about 13 kilometres from Johnson's cabin. Eames didn't want to get to Johnson's cabin by following the direct route along the Rat River. It was an obvious route and one that Johnson would likely expect them to take. This predictability would make it easier for Johnson to ambush his pursuers. As well, a portion of the Rat River runs through a large canyon that is more than 900 metres wide in many places and has banks that are 60 to 185 metres high. The valley is covered with brush. Eames felt that both the banks and the brush would provide a likely cover from which Johnson could shoot at members of the posse.

It was decided that the best route to take was to follow an old trapline along the south side of the Rat River, which went through the woods. Eames wanted to arrive from above Johnson's cabin rather than below it. The group continued on towards the cabin and camped at a spot that their guide, Charlie Rat, said was some six kilometres away from it. The next morning, they packed up and headed towards the Rat

River. But after a while, it became obvious that Charlie didn't know the route very well. It turned out that they were, in fact, nearly 10 kilometres above Johnson's cabin. They spent the rest of the day returning to their camp.

When the men arrived in camp on the night of January 8, Eames realized that they were running out of dog food. They had travelled only 45 kilometres in two days. Getting lost had cost the posse more than just time, it had also eaten away at their supplies. With less than two nights of supplies left and no immediate opportunity to replenish them, Eames knew that he and his men would not be able to wait Johnson out at his cabin. A long siege would not be possible. They would have to get him quickly, making a decisive strike if he didn't surrender on his own. In addition to being weakened by the shortage of supplies, the men and dogs were tired from their trek through difficult weather conditions. Having lost two days retracing their steps to find the right trail had only added to their stress and fatigue.

While the rest of the posse had been retracing their steps, Karl Gardlund and Knut Lang had been sent ahead of the group to see if Johnson was still at his cabin. They made the trek on foot. Careful to stay out of sight, the two men circled the cabin. Smoke was wafting from the chimney. It appeared that Johnson hadn't budged since shooting Constable King. He hadn't taken advantage of the police's absence to flee. Lang and Gardlund made the 22-kilometre trip back to the posse's camp and told Inspector Eames what they had seen. The camp was then moved closer to Johnson's cabin.

On January 9, the nine men and 42 dogs broke camp in mid-morning and advanced. Eames didn't want to take the chance of getting lost again trying to find and follow the old trapline, so the men headed straight along the river. By noon they were within a kilometre of Johnson's cabin. Tying the dogs in the shelter of the woods, they partially surrounded the building.

The location of Johnson's cabin, surrounded by the Rat River on three sides, served to partially protect him. Although he was outnumbered, gunfire could only come from the two sides of the cabin where the riverbank lay, forming a half circle around him. Between the cabin and the riverbank, there was little in the way of cover except for the odd tree and a bit of brush. As one member of the posse later remarked, "You never realize how skinny a tree is until you are trying to hide behind it."

The posse took up its position below the cover of the riverbank, within 20 metres of the cabin. They quietly listened and observed the cabin for signs of Johnson's presence. Smoke was coming out of the chimney and they heard him moving around inside. Concluding that he was at home, Eames called out to him, "Come out, Albert Johnson. We are determined to arrest you." The inspector also explained that King was still alive. This way, Johnson would know the police weren't after him for murder. But there was no response from inside the cabin. Eames repeated the order to surrender and told Johnson that resistance was futile. Again, there was nothing but silence.

Eames knew he couldn't afford to wait. He decided the group's next move would be to break down Johnson's door, and then to run inside and capture the fugitive. Carefully circling the cabin from the cover of the riverbank, Eames crept around and placed his men at strategic points along the sides of the clearing. Gardlund, Lang, and Sutherland used the cover of the high riverbank to fire on Johnson and distract him while Millen and McDowell went over the riverbank to rush towards him.

But Johnson was ready and waiting. As soon as the men had cleared the riverbank, he began firing from the loopholes he had made on every side of his cabin in between the logs.

The men took turns darting towards the cabin, zigzagging across the clearing to avoid the gunfire. Each time they ran past the four-foot door, they tried to pry it open by smashing the butts of their rifles against it. The base of the cabin had a double row of logs with earth packed in between it. Johnson had made about eight holes just above the bottom logs and was using them as loopholes through which to shoot. Despite the bullets, the men kept on running past his cabin. But they were puzzled by the trajectory of his shots. It looked as though Johnson was either lying on the floor as he was firing, or that he was standing in some sort of pit.

Trapper Knut Lang finally succeeded in shoving the

door open, but Johnson spun around and fired at him from a gun in each hand. With the door now open, it was clear that the cabin floor had been dug out; it appeared to be more than a metre below ground level. This created a sort of hole into which Johnson could duck for protection whenever members of the posse would shoot at him. Rifle fire would go over his head, and he would emerge again whenever his pursuers left their cover. Instead of serving as a way into the cabin, the open doorway now gave Johnson another opening through which to shoot — and he used it.

With Johnson firing at him, Lang ran back to the cover of the riverbank and told Inspector Eames about the sunken floor and the two automatic pistols. Then the men heard the trapper slam his door shut. Johnson continued to keep them at bay by shooting through the loopholes in the walls of his cabin. The squat building was small enough to allow him to run from one end to the other quickly, firing at the men by the riverbank.

It was intensely cold. By nightfall the temperature had dropped to –42° C. The air was so bitter that the men couldn't take off their fur mitts to fire their weapons for fear that their hands would freeze — despite the woollen gloves they wore under their mitts. Worse, they couldn't move around to stay warm because they had to keep their positions. Sweat had dampened their clothes and the cold was starting to freeze the clothing to their skin. As more time passed, the men (who were also suffering from lack of sleep) brought the dogs closer to the protection of the riverbank and made a camp. They built a fire and took turns standing by the flames. It was the best they could do to try to stay warm during the stakeout.

Johnson had a distinct advantage: he was protected by the warmth of his cabin while the members of the posse struggled against the frigid temperatures. The longer they stayed, the more food they and the dogs consumed. Eames knew they were running out of time. Flares were lit throughout the night to try to disturb Johnson, but this didn't seem to faze him. However, he would fire at the slightest movement coming from their camp.

At about 9 p.m., Eames realized the posse wouldn't be able to dislodge Johnson by shooting at him and storming his cabin. It was evident from Lang's brief description of the cabin's interior that firing their weapons was pointless since the bullets were going over Johnson's head. The inspector figured it was time to take the next step. He ordered his men to thaw out the frozen dynamite. They tried to do this by warming the individual sticks with their bodies. The results were rather unspectacular, to say the least.

As Johnson and members of the posse continued firing at each other, charges of dynamite were lobbed at the walls of his cabin in an effort to dislodge some of the logs and flush him out, but to no avail. The cold had cut down on the sticks' effectiveness and most of the dynamite didn't even ignite.

By midnight, the flares had gone out. Under the cover of

darkness and the fire of his comrades, Lang climbed over the riverbank and threw some sticks of dynamite onto the top of the cabin. The resulting explosion managed to blow a small hole in the roof and knock off the smokestack, which was covered with two feet of frozen sod. Despite the explosion, Johnson remained undeterred. He seemed to have an unlimited supply of ammunition and continued firing. Lang barely made it back to the safety of the riverbank.

By 3 a.m., Eames had become desperate. It was January 10, his men had spent almost a week trekking from Aklavik, and they still hadn't gotten their man. Eames knew they couldn't stay out much longer. It was cold, supplies were low, and his men were tired. The longer they stayed, the greater the likelihood they would run out of dog food. As Gardlund stood behind him, Eames took out the last four pounds of dynamite and tied the sticks together. Giving it his best pitch, he lobbed the package at the cabin in an arc. The resulting blast blew off the roof, shattered the door, and partly caved in the walls.

Eames thought the size of the blast might have stunned Johnson, even momentarily, and he wanted to take full advantage of it. He and Gardlund rushed towards the cabin. The two men had agreed beforehand that Gardlund would blind the trapper with a flashlight while Eames tried to disarm him. When they got in closer to their target, Gardlund turned on the flashlight and shone its beams into the remnants of the building.

Johnson's cabin on Rat River after being dynamited

But Johnson had heard them coming and was ready. Holding a pistol in each hand, he shot the flashlight out of Gardlund's hand. Surprised, Eames and Gardlund fled back to the cover of the riverbank. Johnson remained steadfast in what was left of his cabin.

Finally, at 4 a.m., Eames called off the 15-hour siege. Before the men headed back to Aklavik, they took one last look at the cabin. The door had been blown to shreds and the roof had been ripped off, but the occupant was still there. They could almost hear Johnson chuckling as they turned away and left. They'd had little sleep in the past 48 hours and had been enduring frigid temperatures for over a week. After the siege was called off, they finally had their first rest in 18 hours and arrived in Aklavik on January 12, minus their quarry.

It was evident to his pursuers that Johnson was a tough customer. He had withstood a marathon siege of his cabin, assaults with 20 pounds of dynamite, and more than 700 rounds of ammunition. He wasn't injured, but his shelter had been destroyed. The crafty trapper realized that the remains wouldn't afford him much protection for long. It was time to flee before his pursuers returned. He knew they wouldn't give up now.

Johnson's best bet was to head out on the land. He stuffed his pack with some camping supplies and as much food as he could carry. Then he grabbed his homemade snowshoes and headed west towards the Yukon border, about 160 kilometres away. Once he reached the Yukon, it was only a matter of travelling another 160 kilometres to reach the sanctuary of Alaska and the United States. There he would be safe from the authorities, at least for a while, since the Mounties wouldn't cross over into another country to chase him down. In the meantime, he would have to rely on his meagre supplies, his wilderness skills, and his wits to keep him one step ahead of the law.

Chapter 5
Manhunt

lbert Johnson was at large and word of the manhunt was getting out to the rest of the continent. Newspapers were covering the story and listeners were glued to their radios. For people throughout Canada, it was a welcome distraction from the Great Depression that gripped the world. Reports were being carried on the Aklavik radio station, and other media outlets were picking them up. "Police Repelled by Maniac's Gun, Prepare for New Attack," proclaimed the *Calgary Daily Herald.* Even people as far away as the United States were starting to hear about the manhunt that was unfolding in the Great White North.

Meanwhile, Eames needed to keep tabs on Johnson and

his movements until a new posse could be assembled to go after him. On January 14, 1932, two days after the first posse had returned to Aklavik, the inspector sent Constable Millen and trapper Karl Gardlund back to the cabin to keep an eye on Johnson.

The two men set out and within a day were hit with an Arctic blizzard that lasted for three days. Despite the difficulties of travelling in this type of weather, they followed the inspector's instructions. After camping a scant three kilometres from Johnson's cabin, they cautiously approached what remained of his home, unsure as to whether or not he might ambush them. With little daylight, the lack of visibility hampered them. But it turned out there was no need to worry. By the time the two men got there, Johnson was long gone. He had vanished on foot, disappearing into the Arctic twilight.

Nearly a week had passed since the siege of Johnson's cabin. After the posse had left, Johnson had taken advantage of the storms and blowing snow to make his getaway. He had used the hard-packed tops of snowbanks to flee, knowing that the blowing snow would more easily erase his footprints and make it harder for his pursuers to pick up his trail. This bought him a bit of time and allowed him to put some distance between himself and the authorities.

Millen and Gardlund crept towards the deserted cabin and poked around the wreckage; the front wall had collapsed and the roof had almost caved in. The two men were amazed that Johnson had not only survived the final dynamite blast on his refuge, but that he had been able to flee afterwards. They searched the area for clues as to where he might have headed. They didn't find any pelts — odd for a trapper — and his cabin revealed no evidence of his identity. There wasn't a document or a shred of paper to give them a clue of who he was or where he had come from. He'd even cleaned up and disposed of his shell casings. Millen and Gardlund couldn't find any prints in the snow indicating in which direction Johnson had fled. The storm had obliterated his tracks.

Knowing that Inspector Eames would soon be joining them with more men to comb the area, Millen needed to get a message to his boss to let him know that Johnson was gone. With limited daylight and no indication of where the fugitive was headed, Millen calculated that the search party Eames was assembling would have to spread out through an area that stretched from the Richardson Mountains in the west to the Mackenzie River in the east. Many men would be needed to cover this 259 square kilometre area.

Since police officers going out on patrol didn't carry two-way radios at that time, Millen had no way to relay messages to the detachment in Aklavik once he was out on the trail. Like other officers, he had to rely on his own ingenuity and survival skills if there was any hint of trouble along the way — there was no means of reaching a fellow officer to rescue him or back him up. The only option that Millen had at the moment was to find someone who could carry a message to Inspector Eames. In an isolated area where neighbours lived kilometres apart from one another, this was no mean feat in the dead of winter. But Millen couldn't wait. He had to let Eames know about the latest development so that the inspector could be prepared. There was also a safety issue to consider. With Johnson on the loose, his pursuers needed to be cautious on the trail — there was always the chance that he might try to ambush them.

Millen set off and eventually came upon a cabin that belonged to a Gwich'in family. The constable explained the situation to the family and the man of the house agreed to take a note to Inspector Eames. As they waited, Millen and Gardlund continued to scour the region whenever the blizzard let up long enough to allow them to do so. They were still trying to figure out what direction Johnson had taken when he'd fled.

While Millen and Gardlund were searching the demolished cabin, Inspector Eames was doing his best in Aklavik to assemble another posse and gather supplies. Constable McDowell had re-injured his knee during the last trip to Johnson's cabin and was now out of commission. The problems with this stranger had cost Eames the services of two of his men.

The Aklavik radio station continued to broadcast the news that Johnson had withstood the Mounties' attack on his cabin and that the RCMP was going after him again. Men and women who were living in isolated cabins swarmed into Aklavik. They were scared that Johnson might visit their homes in search of a place to hide. If the madman was on the loose, the last place they wanted to be was in their cabins, too far from their nearest neighbours to call for help.

Once again, Eames turned to the Royal Canadian Corps of Signals at Aklavik for help. A call went out over the radio asking for volunteers to join the manhunt and help the RCMP catch Johnson. White men and Native trappers stepped forward to offer their services. With the permission of the Department of National Defence in Ottawa, Quartermaster Sergeant Frank Riddell and Staff Sergeant Earl Hersey — both of whom were stationed at the Aklavik radio station — also joined the hunt. Being able to ensure communication between the search party and the base in Aklavik was considered important for obtaining more supplies, more help, or a doctor if necessary. The two military men felt that their radio experience would be an asset to the manhunt. It would allow them to send messages back to Sergeant I. Neary, who would be running the radio station in their absence.

Frank Riddell was a man who seemed more at ease in mukluks than in army boots. He had travelled thousands of kilometres by dog team in the Yukon and the Northwest Territories. Two years after joining the Royal Canadian Corps of Signals in 1922, he and three other corps members had been sent to Aklavik to set up the first radio station there. Their supply ship had sunk off the coast of Alaska and they'd been forced to spend the winter fending for themselves. The group had survived with the help of local Natives, who taught them how to trap, handle dog teams, and travel over ice.

In preparation for joining the hunt for Albert Johnson, signals personnel at Aklavik wanted to ensure that two-way communication between the search party and the base in Aklavik would be possible. Using radio communication out on a patrol had never been attempted before.

The radio operators built a low-power transmitter and receiver and tested it with successful results. Their biggest challenge turned out to be packing this equipment in a compact manner so that it could withstand rough travel on a toboggan and not fall apart going over rough portages.

Riddell also made what he called "goose eggs." He filled the engine cylinders of an old outboard motor with gunpowder. He also filled beer bottles with a mixture of gunpowder and sulphur. Then he inserted a fuse, sealed the bottles, and wrapped them completely with electrician's tape. Riddell figured these goose eggs would come in handy should Johnson decide to hole himself up inside another cabin. If the posse was able to blow a hole in the building, the beer bottles could be thrown in to smoke him out.

By 2 a.m. on January 16, everything was ready. This would be the first time that a two-way radio would be used for police work in Canada. Seven hours later, at 9 a.m., Inspector Eames left Aklavik with eight men to meet up with Millen and Gardlund near Johnson's cabin. Joining him were trader John Parsons (a former member of the RCMP), Special Constable Sittichinli, Quartermaster Sergeant Riddell, Staff

Sergeant Hersey, and civilians Ernest Sutherland, Frank Carmichael, and Noel Verville. The group had plenty of supplies and ammunition. Travelling along the Old Yukon Trail, they hit the same blizzard and temperatures that had hampered the advance team of Millen and Gardlund.

When Eames and the posse arrived at the mouth of the Rat River two days later, they met up with the Native man who carried the message from Millen that Johnson had packed up and fled. Unfortunately, heavy winds had wiped out any tracks that might have helped the men figure out where Johnson was headed. Eames realized that he needed more men to fan out across the area to cover as much ground as possible. The more ground they could cover, the better their chances were of finding some trace of Johnson. Eames recruited 11 Gwich'in men who were camping in the area and they joined the manhunt.

Millen and Gardlund then met up with the rest of the posse, and they all camped along the river, about 15 kilometres above Johnson's cabin. They searched the entire Rat River canyon as far as the Bear River. The men wondered how far their fugitive could have gotten. Surely it couldn't have been too far — Johnson was, after all, facing the same poor weather, but without the benefit of a team of dogs to carry his supplies.

For the next four days, the posse followed Johnson's trapline but they found nothing indicating that he had been there recently. They combed the Rat River canyon, aware that every deserted cabin and clump of trees could provide a

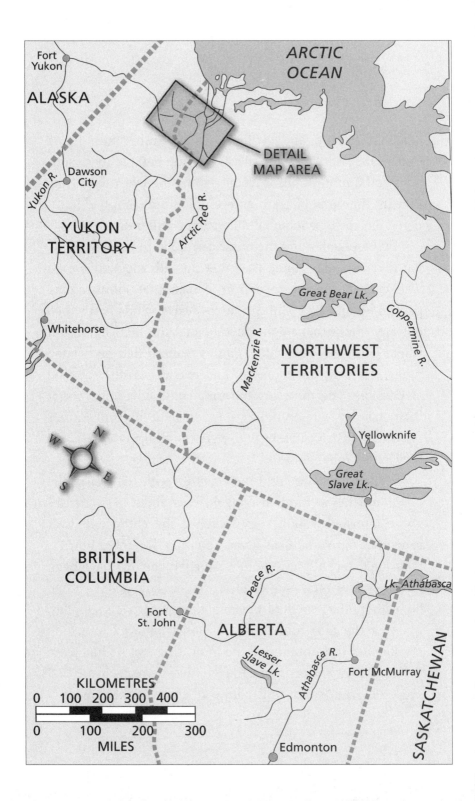

Fort
Yukon

ALASKA

ARCTIC
OCEAN

DETAIL
MAP AREA

Yukon R.

Dawson
City

YUKON
TERRITORY

Arctic Red R.

Whitehorse

Mackenzie R.

Great Bear Lk.

Coppermine R.

NORTHWEST
TERRITORIES

Yellowknife

Great
Slave Lk.

BRITISH
COLUMBIA

Peace R.

Lk. Athabasca

Fort
St. John

ALBERTA

Lesser
Slave Lk.

Athabasca R.

Fort McMurray

SASKATCHEWAN

KILOMETRES
0   100 200 300 400

0   100   200   300
MILES

Edmonton

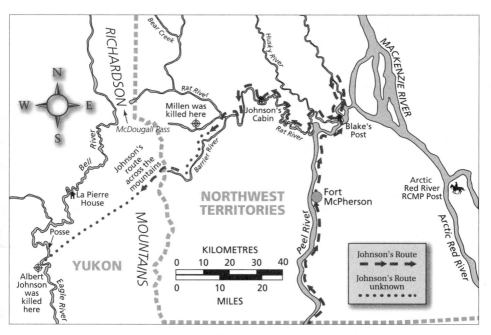

The route of the manhunt through
the Northwest Territories and the Yukon

hiding place from which Johnson could ambush them.

Despite their numbers, Johnson's pursuers faced immense obstacles. These included the extreme cold, blizzards, whipping and stinging winds, and the perpetual twilight of Arctic winters. The group also had great distances to cover in their search for signs of Johnson's presence, and an almost constant need for supplies for both the men and their dogs.

The landscape offered its own challenges. The Rat River valley had thick brush, deep canyons, towering hills, and crooked streams — lots of places to hide. It was covered with willows that were said to be as tall as a man. The easiest way to travel was along the frozen riverbeds. While challenging, the area's terrain also provided Johnson with certain advantages.

For his part, Johnson was a superb outdoorsman and a good shot. While nobody understood his behaviour, they knew that he was making the most of whatever advantages he had. The storms that slowed down the posse continued to erase Johnson's tracks, leaving the men with no clues.

The perpetual problem of dwindling supplies continued to plague Eames. By January 21, it was evident that both the men's food and dog feed wouldn't last long with such a large search party, so the 11 Gwich'in were dismissed. The remaining supplies would be sufficient for nine days, as long as the posse was reduced to four men. It was important that Millen be one of the men to stay behind. Besides being a police officer, he was the only one who had ever met Johnson and could positively identify him.

Eames ordered Riddell, Verville, and Gardlund to stay behind with Millen to continue the search. He told them that they could travel as far as the Yukon–Northwest Territories border. The inspector wanted to prevent the fugitive from going over the divide — Johnson would be easier to catch if he could be contained to the area east of the Richardson Mountains.

The rest of the posse returned to Aklavik, arriving at the post on January 23. Supplies would continue to be hauled to the mouth of the Rat River and Eames planned to replace the four men at the end of the nine days. In the meantime, Riddell's shortwave transmitter and receiver would be used to communicate between the searchers and the base in Aklavik.

As it turned out, the intense cold froze the liquid in the transmitter's batteries. The transmitter would only work from the warmth of a permanent camp where a fire was going. Since the men were out searching the area from daylight until dusk, there was no fire in camp for long periods. This meant that messages could only be sent out intermittently. The camp's location in a deep chasm also made it harder for the shortwave to send and receive signals. The posse was only able to hear transmissions from Aklavik when they were in camp and the batteries had been thawed out.

As Millen and the three other men continued their search, the media continued to cover the manhunt. Radio broadcasts and newspaper stories carried word of Johnson having abandoned his cabin. "Trapper Gives Slip to Mounted Police, Maniac Goes to Hills" shouted the *Toronto Globe*. A headline in the *Vancouver Sun* read, "R.C.M.P. Fights Crazed Trapper," and a headline in the Toronto *Mail & Empire* on January 27, 1932, predicted, "Drama of Arctic Entering Finale." Sales of radios were apparently increasing as people bought them to follow the manhunt. The Canadian North was like a wild frontier for people in the rest of the continent. The dramatic story of one man fending off the Mounties, who "always get their man," was fascinating. How long would he continue to hold out? What was going to happen next? People were staying tuned for the saga's next instalment.

A part-time newspaper correspondent in Aklavik, who worked at the *Hudson's Bay Post*, coined a nickname for Johnson that has stuck to this day. She called him the "Mad Trapper," and the rest of the media joined in. They speculated that he was "insane" and that his behaviour was the product of cabin fever. The *Vancouver Sun* called him "demented." The *Toronto Globe* described him as a "crafty mad hermit," and the *Calgary Daily Herald* referred to him as the "Allegedly Mad Northerner" who was "believed to be 'bush-crazy' from long years of loneliness."

But it was becoming increasingly clear to Johnson's pursuers that he wasn't insane at all. He was wily, had incredible survival skills, and could certainly hold his own in the Arctic. The trapper wouldn't give up easily and the police certainly had their work cut out for them. He was a formidable opponent.

Millen, Gardlund, Verville, and Riddell went back to Johnson's cabin to search it again in case they had missed something the first time. While combing the brush along the Rat River, the men found Johnson's canoe and a cache of supplies hung on a wooden platform in the trees. Since Johnson was on foot and could only carry a limited amount of supplies, they reasoned that he might double back to dig into his cache and then leave a trail. So they found themselves a spot a reasonable distance away and watched the cache through binoculars, waiting in the frigid cold.

But their quarry was too clever to return to the cache of supplies. In fact, he may have deliberately left the supplies there as a ruse to distract his pursuers. The longer the men stayed to watch the cache, the more distance Johnson could put between himself and the posse. Frustrated, the men gave up their surveillance.

They split up into pairs and continued combing the area, spending every precious moment of daylight carefully checking the bush along the Rat River. This was painstaking work. Since they had no tracks to follow, they could only guess where Johnson might be headed. The area was a mess of tangled bush and rivers and tributaries that spun off in different directions. There were lots of places for Johnson to go. The men slowly and methodically worked their way along the Rat River, carefully scanning the snow for footprints that would give them a clue of their quarry's location. But drifting snow, cold temperatures, and little daylight were constantly hampering their search.

Life on the trail was hard. Frost sometimes gathered inside the men's parkas as they combed the area. If they worked up a sweat, their clothes got damp and clung uncomfortably to their bodies. They had to chop wood and build fires to keep warm, cut ice to melt it down for water, feed the dogs, and break up dogfights. After nearly two weeks on the trail, their bedrolls were getting damp. It was no surprise that Noel Verville began developing a cold.

Eventually, the four-man posse found faint but distinctive tracks from Johnson's homemade snowshoes. The tracks were not far from Johnson's cabin, where the Rat and Bear Rivers meet. As the men followed the tracks to the foothills of the Richardson Mountains, which separate the Northwest Territories from the Yukon, they realized that Johnson's trail continued towards the higher hills that hadn't yet been searched. Then they lost the tracks again.

By January 28, the temperature had dropped to –44 degrees Celsius and the posse was out of food for the dogs. Their own food supply had dwindled to very little, but still they plodded on. The men would pair up to search at the beginning of each day and then meet up again at dusk as they headed back to camp. After spending days on end looking unsuccessfully for even the faintest hint of their prey, they were starting to get more than a little frustrated.

While waiting for tea to boil one evening, Riddell went off to see if he could pick up a trail. After wandering around for a bit, he found a faint one and followed it to the top of a ridge. Then he lost it. He circled the area for a while before picking the trail up again in a small creek. Since the trail appeared to be one or two days old, he returned to the camp to tell the others about the relatively fresh tracks he had just found. They were pleased to have a good lead to follow.

The next day they followed the trail that Riddell had found and came upon a few of Johnson's old camps. The distinctive tracks from his homemade snowshoes left no doubt that the camps were his. There was evidence that he had built small fires, perhaps to make tea and to warm up. Because the trail was over hard, windswept ground, the men would often lose it and then find it again, only in sheltered spots. Then they lost it altogether.

After chasing him for two weeks through this cold and unforgiving terrain, the four men were starting to get a pretty good idea of Johnson's habits and patterns of behaviour. He preferred travelling along ridges where even the smallest wind would erase his tracks on the hard-packed snow. He often zigzagged so that he could watch his pursuers from one side of the "z" as they made their way along the other side. This made the men nervous because they realized that Johnson could ambush them. He also liked to create a forked trail. Since the men didn't know which of the two sides of the forked trail might lead to Johnson, they had to follow both sets of tracks to find out. This allowed Johnson to get further away as the posse spent time following empty leads. Soon, he would be within reach of crossing the divide between the Northwest Territories and the Yukon.

Whenever he needed to camp, Johnson would follow a creek until he had reached the protection of the bush. Once he had picked his camping spot, he would continue travelling in a circle and backtrack far enough to see whether he was being followed. He would do this while moving carefully to avoid being detected.

Having run out of leads, the posse was pondering its next move. They had scoured the area but could not find their prey. They were discussing what approach to take when one of the Gwich'in men who had been a member of the search party a week earlier caught up with Millen. He told the constable that two gunshots had been heard from the area around the mouth of the Bear River the previous day. Thinking that Johnson might have taken a chance at being heard in order to replenish his supply of food, the four men retraced their steps to an area they had previously searched. There, in the freshly fallen snow, were Johnson's distinctive snowshoe prints. He had doubled back from the open, rocky terrain of the Richardson foothills and had sought the cover of trees and riverbanks. He wasn't about to make himself more vulnerable by being out in the open where he might be spotted.

To increase their chances of finding Johnson, Verville and Riddell paired up and headed off in one direction, while Millen and Gardlund went in another. It was while travelling in half circles trying to pick up his tracks that Riddell and Verville found a fresh trail and followed it up a small creek. As they followed it, they found the remnants of a caribou. Indeed, Johnson had evidently shot the animal to replenish his food supply. The men followed his trail for a few kilometres, hoping to run into him, until they realized that he was heading back towards his starting point. After cutting across some hills, they found his trail but then lost it again. They started travelling in half circles again as their eyes scanned the ground for foot or snowshoe prints near the confluence of the Rat and Barrier Rivers.

While standing on a ridge parallel to the creek, above a canyon, Verville and Riddell spotted a thin haze of smoke. It was from Johnson's campfire. He was deep in the canyon, puttering around his camp. They could see his fire and the tarp that he had set up, but after two hours of watching they still hadn't spotted the elusive trapper. The two men were feeling the cold from having been virtually immobile for two hours in temperatures of –45° C. With the impending arrival of dusk, Verville and Riddell decided it was too late in the day to attempt to capture Johnson. The darkness could be a liability and they would have a better chance if they waited until daylight. They were also aware that neither one of them had the police authority to launch an attack. So, they headed back to camp to tell Gardlund and Constable Millen that after more than two weeks on the trail, they finally had Johnson in their sights. They would wait until the next day to make their move.

Chapter 6
Shootout

he four men rose early the next morning and set off just after daybreak in the throes of a severe blizzard. The temperature was a chilly –38 degrees Celsius. It was to be their last day out on the trail before they would be replaced. The group followed Johnson's tracks for eight kilometres up a small creek that emptied into the Rat River. The trail ended in a triangular clump of trees and boulders, which provided Johnson with natural fortifications. The group split up and approached his camp cautiously, without being detected. Johnson was in a very deep canyon filled with brush. There was a steep cliff behind him and a sharp hill and creek in front of him. He was more than 30 kilometres from his cabin.

Riddell and Gardlund quietly travelled along the ridge and headed down towards the creek. They positioned themselves across from Johnson's camp, less than 20 metres away from him, looking down into a ravine. From that spot, Riddell could see part of the fugitive's tarp and Gardlund had a clear view of the campfire. They could hear him coughing but still couldn't see him.

Verville and Millen stealthily headed down a slope towards Johnson's camp. Unfortunately, one of them slipped. The resulting noise alerted Johnson to their presence. The men heard him check his rifle and cough but still couldn't see him. He knew his pursuers were there. He was on the alert. As Millen passed through an opening in the trees, Johnson took aim with his .30/30 rifle and fired. Verville and Millen shot back. Johnson then noticed a more protected spot and leapt across his campfire, dropping behind an overturned tree and out of sight of his trackers. In that brief instant, Gardlund caught a glimpse of Johnson and took aim. The sound of the gunshot crashed through the air.

The four members of the posse couldn't see Johnson, but continued to fire blindly towards the camp through a thicket of trees. They hoped that one of their shots would find its target. But there was no response, no more shots from Johnson. Only silence. The men weren't sure whether the fugitive was injured or dead, so they waited. At one point Millen yelled at Johnson to give himself up. Once again there was no response and no movement from Johnson's camp.

But Millen and Gardlund had been present during the siege of the cabin and were well aware of how cunning and dangerous Johnson was.

The four men regrouped under the cover of the snowbank to discuss what to do next. After staying motionless in the bitter cold for a good two hours waiting for Johnson to make a move, Gardlund indicated that he thought he had hit him. With the darkness coming and the temperature continuing to drop, Millen determined that they needed to break the stalemate. The group decided to try to close in on Johnson.

Being careful not to expose themselves out in the open, the men took up their positions. Verville took a spot about 18 metres away, with a downward view over the camp. The others went across the creek and moved to within about 23 metres of Johnson's hideout. With Verville and Gardlund covering them, Millen and Riddell went up the bank to a patch of timber and edged in even closer. Riddell was making his way along the ridge when he saw something sticking out of the snow. As he headed for the cover of a heavy spruce tree, a shot from Johnson's gun whistled past him at very short range and lodged in the bark of the tree. Riddell yelled, "look out" as he dove for cover. After throwing himself onto the top of the bank, he slid over in the deep snow and out of sight.

What Riddell had spotted was the end of Johnson's rifle. Millen, who was behind Riddell, spotted Johnson. He remained on the bank and stood his ground. He got down on one knee and fired. Johnson fired back. Millen fired a second time and Johnson replied with two more shots. With the third shot, Millen stood up, turned around, and fell face down into the snow. His empty rifle dropped down beside him at his feet. The other three men opened fire and Johnson withdrew his rifle. The men were worried about Millen and wanted to get to him to see how badly he was injured. If he was wounded and they didn't move him quickly, he could freeze to death.

Riddell and Gardlund went up onto the bank behind a large spruce tree. From there they could see the spot at the camp, behind an overturned tree, where Johnson was holed up. The two men fired at the spot where Johnson's shot had come from. While Riddell continued firing to ensure that Johnson stayed in his hole, Gardlund crawled through the deep snow on his belly for about three metres, until he reached Millen's feet. Then he undid the constable's bootlaces and tied them together. He used the hastily made handle to drag Millen's body over to the cover of the bank and out of Johnson's line of fire. Verville went to join him and the two men stood over the fallen Mountie, trying to determine whether he was wounded or dead. They examined him, took his pulse, and realized that the bullet had struck his heart, killing him instantly. The "two-gun hermit," as some of the newspapers had called Johnson, had struck again. Constable Edgar "Newt" Millen, 30, from Edmonton had served as a member of the RCMP for 11 years. He was killed about

50 kilometres from where the Rat River flows into the mighty Mackenzie.

The rest of the posse continued to fire into Johnson's camp. Their shots were met with nothing but silence. Daylight was fading and it was evident that they wouldn't be able to flush him out. It was decided that Riddell, who had the fastest dog team, would mush to Aklavik to tell Inspector Eames of Millen's death. Meanwhile, Gardlund and Verville made a platform on which to put Millen's body to protect it from being attacked by any preying animals. Without a dogsled on which to transport him, they were forced to leave his body within less than 30 metres of Johnson's camp. They took Millen's rifle, side arms, snowshoes, and ammunition back to their camp about eight kilometres away.

Just after he'd set off from the scene of the shootout that afternoon, Riddell met Staff Sergeant Hersey and Special Constable Sittichinli. The two men had left Aklavik two days earlier in –44 degree Celsius weather and were on their way to bring fresh supplies to the camp about 40 kilometres up the Rat River. They were also to replace Millen's men. After hearing of the Mountie's death, Hersey decided to join Verville and Gardlund. Sittichinli returned to Aklavik with Riddell — given the poor weather and the perilous conditions on the trail, it was safer for men not to travel alone. The trip wasn't easy. A recent blizzard had obliterated the route in some spots, and there was 64 kilometres of bad trail for every 24 kilometres of good trail.

The rest of the men (Gardlund, Verville, and Sittichinli) made it to their camp at dusk. Gardlund, Verville, and Riddell had been chasing Johnson almost continuously for more than two weeks and they needed some rest and relief from the cold and wet conditions. The terrible weather was taking its toll. Although they had been able to build a fire in camp each night to try to warm up, there had been no real opportunity to dry out their gear. If nothing else, it would be nice to have dry equipment.

Once his pursuers had left his camp, Johnson climbed out of the hole in which he had sought refuge and walked over to look at Millen's body. He quickly realized that he needed to get away before the men returned — for they surely would. Looking around, he saw that there was only one way out. He grabbed some of his gear and collected fistfuls of snow. Then, using his ice axe to carve handholds in the ice and snow, he tackled the vertical cliff behind his camp. After scaling it, the wily trapper sent soft snow cascading down to cover his tracks before vanishing into the frigid Arctic night.

Chapter 7
Slipping Away

iddell and Sittichinli arrived in Aklavik on Sunday morning, January 31, and gave Inspector Eames the bad news about Millen. The local radio station then reported Millen's death to the men and women who lived in the Arctic, as well as to people in the outside world. The murder of one Mountie and the wounding of another continued to draw public attention to the chase that was unfolding in the North.

The manhunt for the Mad Trapper of Rat River was making headlines in newspapers as far away as Toronto and New York. Even the London *Times* was apparently running regular accounts of the chase. "Rat River Madman Kills Policeman, Holds off Others," The Toronto *Globe and Mail* announced on

February 1. "Trapper Kills Police Officer In Gun Battle," the *Calgary Daily Herald* told readers the same day.

It was evident from some of the media coverage that journalists didn't understand just how difficult the weather conditions were in the High Arctic in the middle of winter. Nor did they seem to comprehend just how crafty Johnson was. They wondered how on earth a man who was alone and on foot could possibly outmanoeuvre a posse of Mounties and trappers. Surely the chase would end soon. "Chances of Escape Slight as R.C.M.P. Rush More Men From Aklavik," the *Calgary Daily Herald* predicted.

Newspapers also began depicting the manhunt as a personal battle between Johnson and the police. "Staging a private war of his own against the Royal Canadian Mounted Police, Albert Johnson, demented trapper, fought his third gun battle with police officers Sunday," the *Calgary Daily Herald* recounted on February 1. In another article, the *Vancouver Sun* referred to his resistance as "defiance." On February 2, the *Globe and Mail's* headline referred to "Avenging Mounties." The "lone ranger" depiction of Johnson was garnering public sympathy in southern Canada and other parts of the world for the increasingly elusive fugitive.

As word of Millen's death spread, fear of the madman swept through Aklavik and across the Mackenzie Delta. More and more volunteers from around the region stepped forward to help with the manhunt. Some hitched up their dog teams and travelled over 160 kilometres to Aklavik. They were determined to help the police get Johnson, whatever the cost. People were scared and they wanted him stopped.

Aklavik was a small trading post, but it became a haven for most of the women in the area whose husbands were trappers. They feared that Johnson would visit their cabins while their husbands were on the traplines or off helping the police. Virtually the only woman to stay in her cabin was Noel Verville's wife, who was more than 60 kilometres from her nearest neighbours. She was alone and kept loaded rifles ready in case she needed to use them quickly.

With Johnson so close to the border of the Northwest Territories, police grew increasingly concerned that he might cross over the Richardson Mountains and into the Northern Yukon. People in the area there needed to be alerted to his possible presence. Old Crow, about 200 kilometres west of the search area, had the closest RCMP detachment to Aklavik. As a result of arrangements made at the RCMP headquarters in Ottawa, the officer in charge of the detachment in Dawson, Yukon Territory, had the nearest radio station (which was in Anchorage, Alaska) make a broadcast about the manhunt.

Corporal Arthur B. Thornthwaite, commander of the RCMP detachment in Old Crow, had first heard about Johnson after receiving a radio message saying that King had been wounded. Communications being difficult at that time, the RCMP commander at Dawson had had the information broadcast from the radio station in Anchorage and had followed up with a telegram to Fort Yukon, just across the border in Alaska, in case Thornthwaite had missed the radio message. The telegram cost 35 cents and delivery by dog team was $175.

Thornthwaite sent men out by dog team to warn people in the district not to approach Johnson or try to stop him if he took food. If they saw him, they were to hitch up their dogs as quickly as they could and let the officers at the Old Crow detachment know. A number of the families were out on the land hunting, so the teams had to go quite a distance to warn everyone. Families in the area were scared by the latest news. What if the madman showed up at their camp? Many moved to the safety of Old Crow and La Pierre House.

After hearing about Millen's murder, Constable Sid May and Special Constable John Moses from the Old Crow detachment were ordered to report to Inspector Eames and join the manhunt in the Northwest Territories. They brought along veteran U.S. army sharpshooter Frank Jackson and trapper Frank Hogg. May, who was 26, had only been a Mountie for three years. John Moses had been hired as a special constable at Old Crow in 1929. Originally from Circle, Alaska, he had spent most of his adult life in the Rampart House and Old Crow area. Since he knew the region well, he would be an asset in tracking Albert Johnson.

On the other side of the mountains, in Aklavik, Inspector Eames sent Special Constable Hatting, Reverend Thomas Murray, and trapper Ernest Sutherland to relieve

Gardlund and Verville from keeping an eye on Millen's body and Johnson's camp, and to support Hersey, who was already there. Eames realized that he needed to assemble a bigger party to go after Johnson because the crafty trapper might well try to ambush a smaller group of men if he had the opportunity. As Eames would later write in a report: "I note in press reports that Johnson is referred to as 'the demented trapper'. On the contrary, he showed himself to be an extremely shrewd and resolute man capable of quick thought and action. A tough and desperate character."

Johnson was clever. He was living off the land by setting traps and snares to catch any small animals that he could eat. Larger game, like caribou, would require him to use his rifle. A shot could be heard by searchers and would help them find his location. It wasn't a risk he was prepared to take anymore. He knew that because he had just killed a police officer the Mounties would be stepping up their efforts to capture him. He was confident in his skills, but was also aware that it was only a matter of time before they would catch up to him if he made any mistakes. He couldn't afford to make a wrong move.

Eames wasn't sure that the base camp on the Rat River had enough supplies to sustain a large party. Still, he realized he had little choice but to put together a sizeable posse. Millen's murder had made the situation even more critical and Johnson had to be captured. The inspector made a radio appeal asking every able-bodied man in the district to volunteer, gathering at either Fort McPherson or at Arthur Blake's trading post on the Husky River. They were to bring their guns and enough supplies for themselves and their dogs. Everyone knew that having enough food on hand for the dogs would be a problem. For example, five teams of five dogs each could consume 500 pounds of fish in 10 days.

Eames realized that he was facing a fugitive who had incredible stamina and wilderness skills. He was outmanoeuvring the Mounties and the inspector was starting to feel the pressure. It was getting embarrassing. If they didn't catch him soon, the entire police force would be mocked. Using skis, snowshoes, and dogsleds wouldn't be enough to capture Johnson. It was difficult to travel long distances in the bitter cold, especially through blizzards and over uneven terrain with sleds that were laden with heavy supplies. These challenging travel conditions gave Johnson an advantage on the terrain. Eames was certain that the posse wouldn't be able to catch Johnson through traditional police manhunt techniques.

The only solution was to try something that had never been done before. What Eames needed was an airplane. It would be easier to find the Mad Trapper's trail from the air than on the ground. The plane could travel longer distances more quickly, making it easier to expand the search to cover a wider area. Having a plane would also ease the problem of supplying a larger posse — it could be used to ferry supplies from Aklavik to the men who were out searching the terrain. This would help conserve the men's energy and free them up to concentrate on chasing down Johnson.

One problem with the plan, however, was that taking off and landing in the Arctic could be difficult. In a part of the country where there were no landing strips and the terrain was uneven, there was always a chance that a pilot would have trouble finding a place to set down his plane, or that high winds and blowing snow would keep him from flying at all.

Another challenge Eames faced with his new plan was to convince the powers-that-be that it was necessary. A plane had never before been used in a manhunt in Canada. More than a dozen years earlier, in 1919, the RCMP had discussed and then rejected the idea of having its own air service. Nonetheless, Eames thought it was worth a try. The Mounties were facing a tough customer. They had little choice.

On January 31, 1932, Eames sent a wire to A.E. Acland — commander of the RCMP's "G" division, which operated out of Edmonton — asking that an airplane be employed to join the manhunt. This unusual request was forwarded to the RCMP headquarters in Ottawa. Then it went to the Cabinet of the Canadian government. Eames, however, did not have the time to sit and wait for a response to his request. Instead, he went about assembling an even larger group of men to rejoin the manhunt.

On February 2, 1932, Eames left Aklavik with Sergeant Riddell, Special Constable Sittichinli, former RCMP Constable Constant Ethier, and trappers Ernest Maring and Peter Strandberg. Despite having to face a north wind that was travelling at 50 to 70 kilometres per hour and visibility of no more than 30 metres, the group departed at noon. Along the way to Johnson's camp, they stopped in at Fort McPherson to boost their numbers with Knut Lang and Frank Carmichael. Former Constable Arthur Blake, August Tardiff, and John Greenland were waiting for them at the Rat River. The posse of trappers and current and former policemen had their orders: bring Johnson in, dead or alive.

At 6:30 p.m. on February 2, just hours after Eames and his team left Aklavik, the Aklavik radio station received a message from Edmonton that a plane was being sent to assist in the search. Since Eames had been unable to wait to get word, the station at Aklavik sent out a request to Arthur Blake at Husky River or anyone at Fort McPherson to send a team to meet the inspector at Rat River and give him the message. Then Canadian Airways sent a request to the station asking that two barrels of gasoline be made available at the best landing place on the Rat River. By February 4, the Aklavik station began sending Riddell information about the plane's progress. Meanwhile, six men from the Mackenzie Delta had arrived at Aklavik in response to the radio station's broadcast asking for volunteers to join the manhunt.

Travel for the posse was difficult as they headed towards the camp where Hersey, Hatting, Murray, and Sutherland were waiting. Heavy winds and frequent blizzards meant that progress was slow. Members of the posse often had to run ahead of the dogs to break the trail for them, from Blake's trading post to where the Rat and Barrier Rivers meet. Along the route, a messenger from Aklavik brought the news to Eames that a plane was on its way. Though relieved, the inspector knew it would be a while before the plane arrived. It had to cover 2900 kilometres from Edmonton, and flying hours each day would be short due to the limited daylight and the constant storms that would hamper the plane's progress.

Volunteers were playing a critical role in assisting in the manhunt. Including Gardlund and Verville (who were back in Aklavik taking a well-deserved break), those presently on the trail with Eames, and the four at the camp near the last shootout with Millen, there were now about 17 men tracking Johnson. Eames was the only police officer among them.

On February 5, a week after Millen was killed, the posse met up with the four men who had been guarding Johnson's camp. They surrounded the fugitive's last known hiding place and then discovered that he was gone. All that remained were his bullet-riddled pots and pans. Since they didn't find any traces of blood, they concluded that despite the hail of bullets that had rained on his hideout, Johnson had escaped without being injured.

The rest of the day was spent searching the ravine, which was almost 15 kilometres long. The men were now in the larger foothills of the Richardson Mountains, which had numerous creeks, deep ravines, and canyons running from the watershed. In between the creeks was frozen tundra. It was covered with snow and hardened by unyielding winds

From left to right: Corporal R. S. Wild, Mrs. J. W. Urquhart, Inspector A. N. Eames, Constable A. Milvin, Doctor J. W. Urquhart, unknown.

that continued to blow the snow and obliterate snowshoe tracks or footprints very quickly.

The posse fanned out in small groups to search the area and try to cover as much ground as possible. Johnson's comparatively fresh tracks were found on February 6, 7, and 8 in three different creeks that were 6 to 10 kilometres apart. This showed that he had been crossing over the tundra from creek to creek, probably during the night, and also circling 13 to 16 kilometres back to his own tracks. A night patrol found a set of his tracks that were only a few hours old on the Barrier

River. Then they lost his trail again when it went up to the tundra.

The posse was certain that Johnson was heading towards the Richardson Mountains. These barren, treeless peaks range from 615 metres to 1500 metres high, and the wind chill there can reach –73° C. Natives in the area insisted that no man — white or Native — could cross the divide alone in winter, but Johnson had little choice. With a growing number of men scouring the area, it was only a matter of time before they would catch him. He had been away from his cabin and cache of food for more than two weeks. He was cold, tired, and beginning to get weaker from lack of proper nourishment. His pursuers, on the other hand, had proper food, supplies, and firewood to keep them warm. The dogs would help them to move quickly.

Johnson knew that there was nothing ahead of him but the Richardson Mountains. There was no vegetation for cover, but once over the divide he would be able to head straight for Alaska. All he had to do was continue to outwit and outmanoeuvre them to get there.

Chapter 8
On the Fly

pon receiving government approval to hire a plane to help in the manhunt for Albert Johnson, the RCMP contacted Clennell H. "Punch" Dickins, superintendent of Canadian Airways Limited's western lines, in Edmonton and asked him for help. They needed an experienced bush pilot who understood the difficulties of flying in the North in the middle of winter, where weather conditions could include fog, wind, and snow, and where the mountainous terrain made it challenging to find a flat surface on which to land.

Dickins was familiar with the North. In 1928, he won the McKee Trophy for outstanding achievement in aviation. He was given the award after completing an unprecedented flight that took him from Winnipeg up and across large, unexplored areas of the Northwest Territories, and then back to Winnipeg. He had made this 6400-kilometre trip in 37 hours of flying time over a period of 12 days. It would have taken more than 18 months to cover the same area by dogsled.

After giving it some thought, Dickins decided to send his accomplished chief pilot, World War I veteran Wilfrid "Wop" May, to join the manhunt for Johnson. It was May who the legendary Red Baron, Manfred von Richthofen, had been chasing when he was shot down and killed during the war. May had gone on to down 13 enemy planes and was awarded the Distinguished Flying Cross in 1918.

Like Dickins, May had experience flying in the North. On January 2, 1929, he and Vic Horner had flown on a mercy mission to Fort Vermilion, Alberta, to bring an antitoxin serum to two trading posts in order to prevent a diphtheria epidemic. A man from one of the posts had mushed nearly 250 kilometres in two weeks to reach the closest telegraph office, which was at Peace River, to send word that one person had already died and others were sick. Dogsleds would have taken too long to transport the serum and an entire community could have died waiting. May and Horner had needed to arrive quickly in order to save lives in the two isolated communities.

Their flight had been made in a plane with an open cockpit — not exactly suitable for winter weather. Nonetheless, they had covered more than 960 kilometres over sparsely populated territory. Although the serum had been wrapped in a woollen blanket, keeping it warm in the relentless wind and temperatures of –33 degrees Celsius had been a challenge. They'd used a charcoal heater aboard the plane to keep it from freezing. The pilots, however, hadn't been quite as successful in keeping themselves warm. By the time they'd finally arrived at Fort Vermillion, they were so numb and frostbitten that they had to be lifted from the plane. Still, their mercy mission had been a success. The serum they'd brought arrived in time to save both communities. No one else had died. Later in 1929, May and another pilot, Idris Glynn-Roberts, had arrived in two Bellancas on the first mail run from Edmonton to Aklavik. There was no doubt that the 35-year-old May could handle his plane in the North.

On February 2, 1932, Captain Wop May was at his home in Fort McMurray, northern Alberta, when he received a telegram from Dickins requesting that he fly to Aklavik to join the manhunt. The Mounties needed him to transport supplies and personnel as well as to look for Johnson's tracks from the air. May had been following the search in the newspapers and had been able to tune in to hear the latest reports from the radio station in Aklavik. When he got the telegram, he was ready to help.

It was about –34° C when Punch Dickins flew to Fort McMurray the next day, along with an RCMP member and a supply of tear gas bombs from the police in Edmonton. May was already in his plane with the engine running when his

Wilfred Reid "Wop" May (left), pilot, and Jack Bowen, airplane mechanic

boss landed. They quickly transferred the supplies to May's Bellanca monoplane. (This was the same type of aircraft that American pilots Clarence D. Chamberlain and Charles Levine had used in June 1927 to make the first non-stop flight between New York and Germany, a distance of 6257 kilometres, in 43 hours, 49 minutes, and 33 seconds.) Then Constable William Carter, who was heading north to replace Millen, came aboard the aircraft with May and his mechanic, Jack Bowen. May gunned the engine and they took off on their 2400-kilometre flight to Aklavik.

At first, the weather was good as they flew at 192 kilometres an hour. Then they began hitting snowstorms, which made visibility difficult. By the time they reached Fort Smith, just inside the border of the Northwest Territories, a blizzard was tearing its way towards them. They had completed 424 kilometres and May decided that it would be best to spend the night in the community rather than risk having to make a forced landing just beyond it.

Although it was –34° C and the weather wasn't looking promising, May decided to keep going the next day. More than an hour later, he and the rest of the party aboard the plane were ploughing their way through a blizzard. They could barely see where they were going, but managed to reach Fort Simpson by noon and landed there for the day. They had travelled 744 kilometres since leaving Fort Smith that morning. May was well aware of the dangers the perilous weather posed north of the 60th parallel.

Storms sometimes forced planes to land unexpectedly in the middle of the tundra, far from the nearest settlement. (In September 1929, pilot Tommy Thompson had been flying the president of a mining company and seven others from Baker Lake to Bathurst Inlet. They had been forced to land during bad weather, setting off a search that had involved 15 pilots, including Punch Dickins. Nearly two months had passed before the searchers had gotten word that Thompson's plane hadn't had enough fuel to continue its journey.)

Though the thermometer had dropped to –43° C and

the weather conditions were still poor the next morning, May decided to keep going. He understood the difficulties the Mounties were facing in trying to catch Johnson, and he was eager to reach Aklavik to join the manhunt. The 480-kilometre trip to Fort Norman (now Tulita) was one of the worst that May had ever experienced. Winds were gusting at 55 to 65 kilometres per hour. May later described the conditions in an article published in *True Detective Mysteries* magazine in October 1932: "We bucked snowstorms and terrific north winds all the way down the river. Near Fort Norman, at four thousand feet, the wind had increased to hurricane force. Although, at times, I had my throttle wide open, we were being blown backward over the ground; and then a blizzard blotted out the earth and left us bumping about up there, completely blind." The three men were relieved when May finally set down the Bellanca in the midst of the storm. It had taken them four hours to complete a journey that should have taken them about two and a half.

On February 6, May and the others got up and dug their plane out of the snow so that they could make the final leg of their trip. Although it was still −43 degrees, the storm had spent its fury. The men made their way to Arctic Red River, where they were told to meet Inspector Eames and his posse at their camp at the mouth of the Rat River. After a few unsuccessful attempts to locate the posse, May saw no sign of them and continued on to Aklavik for the night. The Aklavik radio station radioed the search party on the ground to let them know that May, Constable Carter, and Jack Bowen had arrived.

A blizzard was swirling towards Aklavik the next morning. Once again, May and the rest of the men had to dig the plane out of the snowdrifts. Just before noon, the storm had eased up enough for the plane to take flight. May left Aklavik with Constable Carter and Dr. J.A. Urquhart aboard, then flew through the snow flurries towards Eames's camp at the mouth of the Rat and Husky Rivers. Dr. Urquhart had volunteered to fly with May that day in case there were other casualties and medical assistance was needed. He was well aware of just how dangerous Johnson was — he was the doctor who had cared for Constable King when the officer was rushed to the hospital in Aklavik.

Soon, May spotted four members of the posse creeping up on one of Johnson's old camps on a creek near the Barrier River. They were being cautious in case Johnson was nearby. However, once they realized he was gone, they straightened up. May landed on the tundra three kilometres away and delivered much-needed dog feed. He left Constable Carter with the search party and made arrangements to bring more supplies from Aklavik.

Next, May flew over the area that lay ahead of the party. Flying low to the ground, he followed Johnson's trail for about eight kilometres up the Barrier River. He spotted tracks on the side of a mountain and there was no doubt that they belonged to Johnson. The fugitive's bulky homemade snowshoes left a distinctive print, showing an unusual twist on one foot. With the light getting bad, May followed the posse's tracks to the camp at the Rat River and spent 15 minutes looking for a place to land. He finally found a tiny spot between two hills. Although his plane had skis, finding a place flat enough on which to touch down between rivers, creeks, hills, and canyons would continue to be a challenge for May during the search.

That evening, the station in Aklavik radioed the information about Johnson's tracks to the search party on the ground and Riddell acknowledged the message. He had spent the entire day in camp fiddling with the transmitter and now it seemed to be working. The crew at the radio station in Aklavik could hear him. With two-way communication established, Wop May was pleased to know that he could successfully relay information to the ground party.

After spending the day with the bush pilot, Dr. Urquhart realized just how much of an asset the plane was to the manhunt; it travelled fast enough that it would be able to fetch him, or bring any injured members of the posse to the hospital in Aklavik quickly. It was decided that he would stay on standby at the settlement in case his services were needed.

The next day, on February 8, the pilot took off from Aklavik at about 10:30 a.m. in temperatures of −43° C and flew through the mountains to bring a load of food and dried fish for the dogs into the camp, which was located on the top of a bare, treeless mountain just east of the Yukon border. The men were living in canvas tents in the brush along the Rat

River. Small stoves kept them warm and they slept on caribou skins under their eiderdowns, as was the custom in the Arctic. When May arrived, the drifting snow almost covered the tents.

About 20 men were out on the patrols leaving the camp, and they were covering a wide area. With May now bringing supplies to the searchers, the men could better concentrate their efforts on trying to find Johnson. They no longer needed to worry about sending men and dog teams to Aklavik to bring back sufficient supplies — a trip that would take dog teams a few days but took May less than an hour.

With the supplies safely delivered, May flew off over the divide between the Northwest Territories and the Yukon to the headwaters of the Rat and Bell Rivers to see if he could spot the tracks he had seen the day before. "It was very hard to see, as there was no sun," May later recounted. "You can't see anything, everything is white and it was very hard to pick up anything."

Riddell knew the area well, so May took him up in the plane to show him where he'd seen Johnson's tracks. Despite low-lying clouds and gusting winds, they found them again. In one place, a trail headed towards the divide between the Northwest Territories and the Yukon. Another went along the Barrier River and ended abruptly in some bush. They later spotted a faint trail going from there and ending in a circle. It was evident that Johnson had backtracked and camped off the main trail to be able to keep an eye on it from a distance.

In a matter of minutes, May had scanned an area that would have taken the ground party more than a day to travel. From their vantage point overhead, he and Riddell were able to see which trails were false leads designed to keep the trackers distracted while the Mad Trapper moved on.

Johnson had made his way through the canyon and some bush that four members of the posse had been searching when the plane had first arrived. Then, after travelling along the open tundra for a while, it appeared that he'd hit another creek and had followed it until he'd reached the Barrier River. He had then followed the river until he'd reached its head, at which point he'd circled back on his trail and had made a place to camp in some timber.

After that, it looked as though Johnson had headed back to his old trail and had travelled up a creek leading to the continental divide that splits the Northwest Territories and the Yukon. It was clear that at one point he had been only about six kilometres above his pursuers' camp. The men in the plane knew that this had not been an accidental close call on Johnson's part. Ever vigilant, he had climbed up on to a high ridge and had looked around very carefully. Johnson always made sure to know where his pursuers were and just how close they were getting.

After circling the area for an hour, May and Riddell landed and told Eames what they had seen. The inspector ordered that the posse's base camp be moved closer to where Johnson's tracks had been spotted, at the place where the two freshest trails intersected. The ground search was intensified.

On the return trip to Aklavik, May stopped at the creek where Millen had been shot more than a week earlier. He loaded the constable's frozen body onto his plane and brought it back to Aklavik. His body was placed in the RCMP guardroom, where it stayed until his burial in Edmonton.

As May and Riddell were following Johnson's tracks from above, more volunteers were joining the posse below. On the afternoon of February 8, Constable Sid May (no relation to Captain Wop May), from the Old Crow detachment, reported to Inspector Eames, accompanied by Special Constable John Moses, trapper Frank Hogg, and Frank Jackson, who operated the trading post at La Pierre House. The four men had travelled from La Pierre House and over the mountains from the Yukon.

Even though it was a warmer –31° C, high winds grounded Wop May's plane on Tuesday, February 9. But the posse kept hunting. One patrol, led by Constable May, searched the area around the Barrier River. Just before returning to their camp, Special Constable Moses spotted Johnson's snowshoe tracks and noticed that they were headed towards the divide. Once again, the posse could only conclude that Johnson was about to make a desperate bid to scale the Richardson Mountains and cross into the Yukon when the winds were strong enough to erase his tracks.

Eames decided to follow Johnson into the Yukon as soon as Captain May was able to drop off enough supplies for the searchers to make the trip. When the inspector asked for volunteers, he had no trouble finding people willing to accompany him. They were all well aware of the difficulties that lay ahead. The Richardson Mountains are an extension of the Rockies. But they are so far north that they are virtually devoid of the brush that can offer protection from the high winds and storms that sweep across their barren peaks. Anyone climbing them in winter must bring wood to build a fire. With temperatures that can drop to −73° C with the wind chill, frostbite was a very real risk.

While Constable May, Moses, and Jackson stayed behind at the Barrier River camp, the rest of the group decided to set up a camp back to the mouth of the Rat River. It would be easier for Captain May to land there and bring them supplies.

Although the weather wasn't much better the next day, Captain May and Bowen dug the Bellanca out of the snow and took off. It was −45° C and winds swept snow to a height of 300 metres, making it impossible for the pilot to see the ground and land his aircraft. When he flew over the Rat River, May found a gale blowing through the pass. He returned to Aklavik at 11 a.m. Three hours later, the weather conditions weren't much better and the gale had gotten worse, but May tried again. He was forced to drop the load of supplies off at the mouth of the Rat River near the Husky River. Then he returned to Aklavik once again.

On the ground, the heavy snow kept the posse in camp

that day. While they waited for the weather to clear, the clock ticked away. Waiting out the weather was costing them precious time and making it harder to get close to Johnson.

Despite the terrible weather conditions, an article published in the *Toronto Globe* on February 11, 1932, sounded optimistic. "Johnson's warfare with police is nearing the end, police officials here believe. Since he has been away from his dynamite-shattered cabin for more than two weeks, he cannot have much food left, and the search has been intensified, they point out, to such an extent that the trapper is almost certain to be surrounded by the posse within a few hours, anyway."

The public and the media continued to stay glued to their radio sets for the latest news on the increasingly intense hunt for the Mad Trapper. They wondered about the man who was keeping the Mounties at bay. One newspaper printed a front-page story and photo of Albert Johnson. Unfortunately, they soon discovered that it wasn't the same Albert Johnson. The Mad Trapper's namesake, a resident of the Princeton district of British Columbia, angrily went to the newspaper's office to complain. He said that the man in the photo was him, not the one being chased around the High Arctic. Although he had spent time trapping up in the Northwest Territories, he wasn't the Mad Trapper and was certainly not wanted by the police. The newspaper was forced to print a retraction.

The sky was fairly clear in the search area on February

11, and despite heavy winds, Captain May was able to drop off more supplies, as well as Joe Verville (Noel's brother) to bolster the size of the posse. By that time, the party on the ground had managed to piece together Johnson's trail bit by bit. It had been painstaking work since the winds had erased his tracks along the hard-packed snow in many places.

With Constable May and his party joining the manhunt, Eames was beginning to realize that the group was getting to be too large to travel together efficiently. The inspector knew he wouldn't be able to get enough supplies together to go over the divide into the Yukon with so many people. He waited several days, until Captain May had brought a sufficient amount of supplies to the base camp, before splitting up his group.

The weather was better on Friday, February 12, and Captain May was able to cover 120 kilometres of mountain flying around the Husky River area. When he returned to the mouth of the Rat River late in the day, Eames, Carter, Riddell, and Gardlund were waiting for him. Now that they had enough supplies at the camp, Eames, who had already decided that he would send searchers over the mountains and into the Yukon in the morning, discussed with his men how to proceed. Judging from Johnson's tracks, he was weakening, but was still two days ahead of his pursuers.

While the men were talking, Constable May and Peter Alexie arrived at the camp on the Rat River. Alexie, a Gwich'in man, had travelled 145 kilometres non-stop by dog team from La Pierre House in 16 hours. He had left that morning at 6 a.m. and it was now 10 p.m. Excitedly, he told Inspector Eames that a group of Natives had spotted strange snowshoe tracks about three kilometres east of La Pierre House. They had been out hunting when they'd seen Johnson's distinctive tracks crossing the very ones they had made that morning. Everyone in the area was scared. If the Mad Trapper was in the district, how safe were they? A number of people had abandoned their traplines and camps in the bush and had fled to the safety of the trading post. (La Pierre House, which sat on the Bell River, was so isolated that it took four years to ship out furs and bring in supplies.)

It didn't seem possible that Johnson had travelled 145 kilometres in three days, but from the description of the snowshoe prints, the group concluded that he had indeed. It was now evident that Johnson had climbed the barren and seemingly impassable Richardson Mountains during the high winds and low temperatures of the previous few days, and that he had gone quite a distance. With the wind chill, the temperature at the top of the 1500-metre peaks could plunge to 100 below. Eames was astonished that a man who had been living off whatever small animals he could snare for the past month, and who was hauling his own supplies on his back, would even attempt this dangerous move — in the middle of a blizzard, no less. He would likely have had to spend a night on the mountain, in the frigid temperatures. It was an extremely risky move, one that other men wouldn't have attempted. Johnson's strength and stamina seemed almost superhuman.

There was no point in having the entire posse travel through the mountains to La Pierre House. Eames decided to split the group into two. He assigned eight men to make their way to La Pierre House by dog team, following Johnson's trail. Eames then had Captain May bring eight pairs of snowshoes that were appropriate for soft snow and gave them to Staff Sergeant Hersey, Constable Sid May, Special Constables John Moses and Lazarus Sittichinli, and civilians Constant Ethier, Frank Jackson, Peter Alexie, and Joe Verville (who was replacing brother Noel, who had a bad cold). Then he, Riddell, Carter, and Gardlund flew back to Aklavik to replenish their supplies and fly on to La Pierre House. They hoped to intercept Johnson.

The next morning, the plane left Aklavik with Inspector Eames, Carter, Riddell and Gardlund aboard and arrived at La Pierre House at about noon. The Jackson Brothers' Trading Post would be their new headquarters for the rest of the manhunt. Contrary to the hard-packed terrain of the Northwest Territories, the snow in the Yukon was soft and deep. After landing, Captain May had to run the Bellanca up and down the landing strip for half an hour to pack down the snow and create a runway from which he would be able to take off.

It was snowing heavily and the visibility was too poor for May to try to scout out Johnson's tracks from the air. The men in the plane couldn't find his trail heading over the divide because the high winds had blown the snow clear of the tundra. Nonetheless, there was no doubt in anyone's mind that Johnson had crossed over into the Yukon, probably through the Barrier River Pass. They later found his trail in the hillsides that sloped gently down into the Bell River. Then, studying the trail they had been told about by Alexie, they were certain it was Johnson's.

It was increasingly evident to his pursuers that Johnson was a first-class bushman with incredible smarts and stamina. As Captain May later told a Scout troop in Calgary, Alberta, "His tracks could be seen in one place tonight and then tomorrow morning they would be seen 20 or 30 miles away. He travelled that distance in one night."

With his pursuers getting closer and closer, Johnson had had little choice but to tackle the divide that the Native peoples in the area had said was impossible to cross alone in the dead of winter. But the terrain and weather conditions were different in the Yukon. The soft and deep snow made footprints more evident and there was little wind to erase them. Now it would be easier for his pursuers to pick up his trail as he reached the Bell River and passed within 2.5 kilometres of La Pierre House.

Visibility was poor on Valentine's Day and Wop May only had about an hour's window to scout from the air. While he'd been forced to contend with blizzards in the Northwest Territories, he now faced dense fog on the other side of the mountains. Still, he managed to follow Johnson's trail for about 32 kilometres up the Bell River. Then he lost it in a 16-kilometre stretch along the Eagle River, where Johnson had cleverly taken off his snowshoes and travelled on foot following the tracks of a large herd of caribou. When he returned to La Pierre House, Captain May told Eames where he had spotted Johnson's tracks and described a shortcut that the posse could use to get there. This saved the men precious time laboriously searching on the ground and reduced the advantage that the fugitive had gained by crossing over the divide. May then tried to fly to Aklavik to pick up a load of supplies and gas, but he was forced back when he realized that bad weather had sealed off the pass over the mountains.

The group that was travelling by dog team from the Northwest Territories crossed the divide and arrived at La Pierre House on Monday, February 15. They were exhausted from having travelled for three days and carrying heavy loads. They'd had 10 days' worth of supplies for both themselves and the dogs. The deep snow had made travel more difficult, particularly for the dogs to run through, but it had been packed down by a herd of caribou a bit further along. As the posse had struggled through the rugged passes in better weather conditions than Johnson would have experienced days earlier, they had been cheered by the thought that Johnson would be easier to track on this side of the border, where the land was flatter, the snow was softer, and there was little wind to erase his tracks.

By the time the larger posse arrived at La Pierre House,

Eames, Carter, Riddell and Gardlund had already set out on foot. So, the rest of the men headed up the Bell River to join them. They found Johnson's trail amidst the caribou tracks and followed the tracks up the Eagle River. It was evident from his trail that Johnson was getting more and more tired and weak. He seemed to be staggering, and his prints often zigzagged. He had been away from his cabin for about a month now and was beginning to slow down. The lack of food and sleep was surely catching up with him. Judging by his abandoned camps, it also appeared that he no longer had food. He survived by snaring squirrels and brewing tea over tiny fires hidden in small caves in snow-covered riverbanks. "You could see where he was slowing down from his tracks," Captain May recalled. "He was not going straight."

As the ground team followed Johnson's tracks, Wop May and Bowen spent three hours digging out their plane. They managed to make it to Aklavik this time and returned to La Pierre House with seven ten-gallon drums of gas and eight gallons of oil and supplies.

Dense fog and poor weather grounded May's Bellanca the next day, but the searchers were out scouring the Bell and Eagle Rivers for signs of Johnson. They studied his tracks and estimated them to be about a day and a half old. Gardlund and Riddell cut spruce trees and made arrows in the snow so that Wop May could see from overhead which route to follow once the weather cleared. That night, the men stopped to camp about 24 kilometres from the mouth of the Eagle River.

They sensed that they were finally closing in on the fugitive who had eluded them for nearly seven weeks.

Around the same time that the posse felt they were nearing Johnson, men in Old Crow wanted to form a posse of their own in case the Mad Trapper went down the Porcupine River. However, a shaman elder from the Old Crow band told them not to. "You no go look. One sleep and he die."

Chapter 9
The End of the Trail

he men in the posse woke before dawn on the morning of February 17. Eager to finally get Johnson, they didn't waste any time getting ready. The group, consisting of eight men with dog teams and another three on foot, wanted to have enough time to travel a good distance. There was also a certain degree of concern that trapper Phil Branstrum hadn't been warned about Johnson. He had a cabin nearby and the searchers wanted to reach him before the desperado did.

Nobody knew exactly where Branstrum's cabin was located, so the posse needed to give itself as much time as possible to try to find it. They had planned for Wop May to look for it from the air, but the pilot hadn't been able to get off the ground at La Pierre House the day before because of intense fog. May was still having trouble with fog, but the sky was starting to clear. Despite the darkness, the men picked up Johnson's relatively fresh tracks again, which appeared to be less than 24 hours old. Johnson couldn't be far away. They began following the tracks about 40 kilometres from where the Eagle River intersects with the Bell River.

Just before noon, Albert Johnson was making his way along the snaking Eagle River. He climbed a tree and looked out over the area to plan his route. Thinking that the posse was ahead of him, he climbed back down and walked along the river for nearly a kilometre. At the same time, Staff Sergeant Hersey was driving the first dog team. He was approaching a sharp bend in the river when he spotted a man standing only 270 metres away. Although he had been chasing the Mad Trapper for about a month, he had never actually seen him. At first Hersey thought it was another trapper in the district. Then the man with the heavy backpack reached back and grabbed his snowshoes. Hersey recognized their distinctive shape and realized that he had finally come face to face with the fugitive who had been on the lam for seven weeks.

Johnson had been trying to backtrack, not realizing that his pursuers were so close behind. He looked up and was visibly surprised to see Hersey facing him. After quickly shoving his feet into his snowshoes and lacing them up, Johnson grabbed his rifle and dashed towards the riverbank, then around a point in the bend of the Eagle River.

Hersey grabbed his own Lee Enfield rifle from his sled and dashed towards the centre of the river. He yelled at Johnson to surrender. Johnson ignored him and tried to run straight up the riverbank, which was about nine metres high. Hersey knew that it would be dangerous, even deadly, if Johnson reached the top of the riverbank. It would put him in a strategic position to pick off his pursuers one by one. Hersey fired at Johnson's packsack three times, sending the outlaw slipping down the riverbank each time. Joseph Verville, who was driving the second team, joined in.

Constable Sid May, Karl Gardlund, and Frank Jackson were the next ones to arrive on the scene. Word was being passed back through members of the party that Johnson was just ahead. The bend in the river was such that they still couldn't see him. As they advanced, the men followed one another onto the scene that was unfolding.

Dropping down on one knee in the middle of the river, Hersey took careful aim at Johnson's shoulder with his .303 to wound him. The posse still wanted to try to capture him alive. Being a marksman, the staff sergeant wouldn't miss at such a short distance. He was kneeling on his right knee with his left elbow resting on his left knee. He'd barely had a chance to squeeze the trigger when Johnson reached for his .30/30 rifle, turned around, and fired.

Hersey felt a searing pain as the bullet grazed his kneecap and entered his elbow, and then he toppled over. He was conscious and the wound to his knee was causing him a great deal of pain. He couldn't move from the waist down but wanted to make sure that Johnson didn't hit him again. Using his arms to dig in the soft snow, he made a small hole into which he could burrow.

By this time, the rest of the posse had rounded the bend in the Eagle River and was on the scene. Constable May indicated that the posse should spread out on either riverbank and surround Johnson. Two men positioned themselves on the bank just above the fugitive, but he was too busy watching Hersey to pay them any attention. He fired three more shots at the wounded man, but missed. Some of the men were running along the riverbank ahead of Johnson, nine metres above him, and firing. With Johnson's attention now diverted elsewhere, Joe Verville went over to look after Hersey, placing him in a sleeping bag to keep him from freezing.

Johnson suddenly stopped firing and began running back up the river. He was backtracking away from the party and stopping every 50 metres or so to look, listen, and shoot at his pursuers. He was heading towards the riverbank opposite the one he had just left. It wasn't as steep and he hoped he'd be able to reach the top this time.

Members of the posse were now in position, some spread on either bank while others were firing at him from the centre of the river. Gardlund, Jackson, Moses, and Ethier were one side. Sittichinli, Carter, Alexie, and Riddell had gone along the other side. Eames and Constable May stood in the middle of the river and called three times for Johnson to surrender, but he ignored them and kept on firing. Inspector Eames heard some of the men shout, "This is your last chance to give yourself up." Johnson responded by shooting at his pursuers with his rifle.

With bullets whizzing around him, Johnson was unable to reach the bank and the cover of the brush. He threw himself down in the centre of the river and burrowed into the soft deep snow, lying on his side and shielding himself with his heavy pack. He had sustained a leg wound when a bullet had struck a box of ammunition in his pocket and the resulting explosion had blown a hole in his hip.

He was also struck in the shoulder and in the side, but started firing again and kept it up for 10 solid minutes. Johnson was completely surrounded, and a few men were firing on him from above. They were shooting to injure him, not to kill, but he wouldn't let up. Special Constable Moses poked his head over the top of the riverbank to look, but Johnson detected the movement and took aim. Moses and two others then began to fire again, but Johnson didn't respond. Trapper Frank Jackson ran out of ammunition during the gunfight and decided that he could best be of help by directing the men's shots. He climbed out from a bush under which he had been lying and then calmly walked up the riverbank to a good vantage point. He began ranging, calling "a little high" or "a little low" to indicate where the men should aim. All the while, Johnson was still lying in the middle of the river.

As the gunfight was taking place on the ground, Wop May and Jack Bowen arrived from La Pierre House. They circled overhead, watching and taking pictures of the action unfolding below. From their vantage point, the participants were nothing more than moving black dots, but the flashes of weapons being discharged were very clear. May and Bowen could also hear the sounds of gunshots over the noise of the plane's engine. They noticed someone lying in the snow and realized that a member of the posse had been hit. May had bombs aboard his plane but couldn't drop them on the trapper because the other men were too close.

Some 20 minutes after Johnson had burrowed into the snow, Wop May noticed that he was no longer shooting back and that his body was sprawled awkwardly, face down. His right arm was stretched out, still holding his rifle. Detecting no movement, the pilot swooped low and tipped his wings to signal to the posse that it looked like the chase was finally over.

Under the cover of fire from the others, Constable May slowly and cautiously moved towards Johnson. He turned him over and saw from his frozen features that he was dead. Johnson had taken seven bullets to the legs, back, and shoulders. The fatal shot had passed through the small of his back, severing his spine. He had died while lying on his side, reloading his rifle. "There was no chance for him to get away," Riddell later recalled in a CBC Radio interview.

It was 12:10 p.m. on February 17 — 49 days after

Constable King was shot — and Johnson now lay dead on the ice, 24 kilometres from the mouth of the Eagle River. What had started out as a routine call had ended with the deaths of two men and serious wounds to two others. Albert Johnson had battled freezing temperatures, hunger, and blizzards for five weeks. He had travelled some 240 kilometres through difficult terrain and spent at least one night in the windy and treeless mountains that separate the Northwest Territories and the Yukon. He died about 270 kilometres from the Alaskan border with just a dead squirrel for food. But it had taken seven Mounties, three special constables, and more than 30 civilians to track him down. He had desperately resisted to the end.

Gardlund, who had been at Johnson's cabin during the 15-hour siege five weeks earlier, positively identified him. John Moses was pretty sure that his shot wasn't the one that had killed Johnson, but he later threw away his gun. He didn't like the idea of eating meat from an animal that was killed using the same gun that may have killed a man.

Once the gun battle was over, some of the men went to break up a dogfight that had erupted during the shootout. There were eight teams, six dogs per team, and the men had a difficult time untangling the harnesses and sleds. Other members of the posse turned their attention to Hersey. Riddell was overjoyed to see that he was still alive. Hersey was bleeding from his knee and arm, but was still conscious. He appeared to have been hit three times.

Captain May landed his Bellanca within a few metres of where Hersey lay. Riddell and Jackson, who were by the wounded man's side, couldn't do much to help him. May took out a medical kit that he carried aboard his plane, bandaged the wound, and gave Hersey a sedative to ease the pain. While Riddell got his army buddy ready for the journey ahead, Wop May walked over to the crowd gathered around Johnson.

They stared down at the emaciated body and gaunt features. Johnson's arms, legs, and feet had been frozen repeatedly. Though he'd only weighed about 145 pounds at the time of his death, he had been carrying heavy snowshoes that weighed about 10 pounds each and a pack that weighed almost 150 pounds. What was most shocking about Johnson's appearance was the expression that was frozen on his face in death. His lips were curled back in an ugly sneer, and his teeth looked like fangs sticking out through his beard. Johnson hadn't found the peace in death that had eluded him in the last weeks of his life.

Captain Wop May later recalled his reaction when he saw Johnson's face. "I got the worst shock I've ever had. For Johnson's lips were curled back from his teeth in the most terrible sneer I've ever seen on a man's face … It was the most awful grimace of hate I'd ever seen — the hard-boiled, bitter hate of a man who knows he's trapped at last and has determined to take as many enemies as he can with him down the trail he knows he's going to hit."

After looking at Johnson for a moment, Wop May, along with Bowen and Riddell, bundled Hersey into the Bellanca. Riddell sat beside the pilot while Bowen sat in the back with the injured soldier. Hersey complained of pain in his knee, not realizing that he'd also been hit in the chest. The flight from the Yukon to Aklavik wouldn't be easy, however May knew he had no choice but to make it. Hersey would die if they didn't move quickly. May did not want to fly above the mountains because the air was colder higher up, and he was concerned that Hersey wasn't bundled up enough to survive it. Instead, he elected to fly at a lower altitude, weaving through the peaks. Once in the mountains, he was forced to fly through wind and a terrible snowstorm. He couldn't see the sky above him or the ground below, nor could he make out what was on either side of the plane as he manoeuvred his way through the pass at an altitude of 610 metres. May had to rely on his memory to guide his plane and passengers safely through the pass. As he later recalled in the article in *True Detective Mysteries*, "I shut my teeth and let the old Bellanca drone along, and hedge-hopped through. More than once I thought we were sunk when a jagged peak leaped at us through the murk, and whistled past, within a few inches of our wing-tip."

Despite the challenging conditions, the crew made the 200-kilometre flight in 45 minutes and May taxied as close to the hospital as he could. Then the men climbed out to get a stretcher and brought Hersey inside. Dr. Urquhart cut off

Hersey's parka and discovered that one bullet had caused three wounds. After grazing his knee and entering his elbow, it had come out the upper arm, gone into his chest, and hit one of his lungs. It had just missed his heart.

The chest injury had caused internal bleeding and the doctor didn't use any anaesthetic while tying off the arteries to stop the haemorrhaging. If the plane had arrived in Aklavik 15 minutes later, Hersey wouldn't have survived. Dr. Urquhart later found and removed the bullet from just under the skin on the right side of Hersey's back after Hersey complained about a wrinkle in the bed sheets. May waited on standby in case he had to fly Hersey the 2700 kilometres to Edmonton for further treatment, but it turned out to be unnecessary.

After the plane had left the Eagle River with Hersey, Constable Sid May picked up Johnson's body and loaded it onto Verville's dogsled. During the ride back to La Pierre House, the sled rolled over a few times while going over steep banks. When the men reached the community, Johnson's body was wrapped in a tarp and placed in a cache on top of a five-metre-high platform to keep it safe from predators. The next day, Wop May flew back to pick up Inspector Eames and the body of Albert Johnson. The body was placed in the police barracks at Aklavik, photographed, and examined by Dr. Urquhart. The rest of the posse returned to Aklavik by dog team.

Johnson had a baking powder can hanging around his

neck when he died. It contained $2410 in cash. The money was found in denominations of $20, $50, and $100 bills, plus two American $5 bills and one $10 bill. Also on Johnson's person were glass jars containing five pearls, five pieces of gold dental work, and alluvial gold. Other items in his possession included an axe with a handle bearing a bullet mark, a pocket compass, fishhooks, and sewing thread.

Johnson had been an ambulatory arsenal. His firearms collection included a Model 99 Savage .30/30 rifle, an Ivor Johnson sawed-off shotgun, and a .22 Winchester rifle. The ammunition included 39 .30/30 shells, 84 .22 shells, and four 16-gauge shotgun shells. He had no intention of being captured alive. He had saved one final round of ammunition from his rifle for himself.

All that was left of Johnson's presence were the remnants of his cabin, an old canoe, and a carefully concealed cache of supplies. There was no trace of his identity. But everyone was relieved that the manhunt was finally over.

"Mad Trapper Killed After Wounding Pursuer" the headline blared from the front page of the *Globe and Mail* the next day. It was a relief to the families around La Pierre House, as well as those in the Mackenzie Delta, that Johnson was finally dead. The trappers' wives who had sought refuge in Aklavik celebrated. Now they could finally return home. Many people up North had the first good night's sleep that they'd had in a while.

One woman had been alone in her cabin with her

A wooden cairn marks the spot where Edgar Millen died

12-year-old daughter. She would stand in front of her stove stirring food with one hand while holding a loaded gun in the other. When Special Constable Moses told her that Johnson was dead, she instructed her daughter to open the door. Then she tossed the gun out. After having lived day and night with the loaded weapon by her side, she was relieved to be rid of it.

On February 22, Wop May flew back to Fort McMurray, bringing Edgar Millen's body with him. The RCMP constable was buried with full military honours at Beechmont

Cemetery in Edmonton on February 29, 1932, almost a month after being killed. Twenty-nine years later, someone placed a wooden cairn on the spot where he'd lost his life on the Rat River.

Chapter 10
Who was Albert Johnson?

nside the RCMP compound in Aklavik, Inspector Eames fingerprinted Johnson. It was a difficult and gruesome task. The fugitive's body was frozen and his fingers were curled from clutching his rifle to the death. Fingerprints were ordinarily taken while standing behind the person and placing their fingers on the inking pad and paper. This time, the task had to be done twice. The fingerprints were sent to both Ottawa and Washington D.C. in an effort to learn Johnson's true identity. However, police forces in neither country turned up any links to someone with a criminal record.

The rumours of Albert Johnson's true identity have been swirling around since before he met his end on the Eagle

River. It is believed that he ended up in the Northwest Territories by accident, after taking a wrong turn and floating down the Peel River to Fort McPherson. He had been visibly disgusted when he'd realized that he wasn't on the Porcupine River.

In early February 1932, Constable Alfred King, Johnson's first shooting victim, wrote a letter to Constable "Frenchy" Chartrand, who was stationed at Coppermine (now Kugluktuk). King told his friend about the manhunt and said he had heard a rumour that Johnson had been trapping at La Pierre House in the Yukon for two winters and that his partner had disappeared.

Johnson's ability to remain calm under fire, and his skills with firearms, also suggested that he might have had a police or military background. Other people privately speculated that he could have been a Chicago gangster. After all, it was the 1930s and Al Capone was alive and well.

In August 1933, the RCMP learned about a man called Arthur Nelson who resembled Albert Johnson. The man had first appeared in the Yukon in August 1927, and had disappeared in the spring of 1931. He had been a solitary and unfriendly person who had often been seen with a shotgun slung over his shoulder.

Roy Buttle, the manager of the Taylor and Drury Trading Store in Ross River, northeast of Whitehorse, met Arthur Nelson in August 1927 at the trading post. Nelson, who spoke with a slight Scandinavian accent, told Buttle that he was

American and had been raised on a small farm in North Dakota. He claimed that he'd trapped during the previous winter in northern British Columbia, between Dease and Teslin Lakes. And he said that before that, he had worked at the mines in Anyox, British Columbia. Nelson camped about half a mile from the settlement of Ross River and spent nine days there building a boat.

On August 30, 1927, he used the boat to go up the Ross River to an abandoned cabin near Sheldon Lake. He was apparently trapping and looking for gold. After spending the winter there, he went back to Ross River in June 1928. He left a month later, after buying a .30/30 Savage rifle and a few boxes of shells. Johnson's .30/30 Savage couldn't be traced back to Nelson's purchase of the same type of weapon at Ross River because the manufacturer's records had been destroyed.

In August 1928, Nelson was seen in Mayo, in central Yukon, south of Dawson. He went to the Taylor and Drury store and sold his marten skins for $680, receiving the cash from the Bank of Montreal branch there. Two of the $50 bills found on Johnson's body were traced back to the Bank of Montreal branches in Dawson and Mayo.

Nelson left Mayo and returned again in the spring of 1931. He stopped off at a store to buy some supplies, including six boxes of kidney pills. He was seen in Keno in May 1931 and then vanished as suddenly as he had arrived. Johnson was found with 32 pills in his possession when he died nine months later.

Who was Albert Johnson?

Less than two months after Arthur Nelson disappeared from the Yukon, Albert Johnson turned up at Fort McPherson in the Northwest Territories. The physical description, his "lone wolf" attitude, the possession of a Savage .30/30 rifle, and the two $50 bills that were traced back to the Bank of Montreal in the Yukon all suggest that Arthur Nelson and Albert Johnson were the same person. Many who knew Arthur Nelson and saw the photos that were taken of Johnson after he died believed it was the same man, although some couldn't be sure because Johnson was so gaunt.

Over the years, the RCMP has answered many inquiries from people all over the world claiming to be the Mad Trapper's relatives. However, none of the descriptions provided by these claimants has matched Johnson.

Yukon author and historian Dick North has spent 20 years trying to trace Albert Johnson's true identity. That search is detailed in his 1989 book, *Trackdown*. North believes that Johnson may have been John "Johnny" Conrad Johnson, who was born in Bardu, Norway, on July 13, 1898. Johnny Johnson and his family had moved to North Dakota, sailing to the United States just two days after Johnny's sixth birthday. As a young man, Johnson had spent time in three state jails in the United States for a variety of crimes, including armed robbery and stealing livestock. He had come to Canada in the spring of 1923, when he was nearly 25 years old. His family had never heard from him again.

The body of Albert Johnson was never claimed. He was

buried on March 9, 1932, under a spruce tree. For now, the secret of his true identity and why he sparked the largest manhunt in the Canadian Arctic remains buried in his grave in Aklavik. Two stumps inscribed with the initials "AJ" were later placed at the site to mark his final resting place.

Epilogue

A blurred and grainy photograph shows a blond-haired man with stooped shoulders squinting as he stands next to Native missionary preacher John Martin. Riverboat pilot Frank Slim took the photo in July 1930 from the deck of the Drury and Taylor supply boat, the *Yukon Rose*. The blond man in the photo was known as Arthur Nelson — this lone image may be the only photograph of Albert Johnson when he was alive.

Nobody knows just why Johnson went on a murderous rampage that sent Mounties and trappers chasing him over an area of more than 240 kilometres north of the Arctic Circle. But the manhunt, which was also known as the "Arctic Circle War," changed policing techniques. This hunt was the first time that a two-way radio was used to keep contact between an RCMP detachment and officers chasing down a suspect.

The support of an airplane turned out to be the key factor that finally gave the RCMP the edge it needed to catch Johnson. It was the first time that a plane had been used in a manhunt in Canada — and it proved its worth. Although the idea of the RCMP having its own air service had been discussed in 1919, the manhunt demonstrated the important role that airplanes could play in police work. In 1937, the

RCMP formed its own "Air Division" with four DeHavilland Dragonflies. Today, the force uses jets and helicopters. It has aircraft that are equipped with wheels, skis, and floats to enable them to land on a variety of terrain.

Finally, the serious injuries to Staff Sergeant Hersey, from the Canadian Corps of Signals, inadvertently helped to improve medical care. The seriousness of his injuries underscored the need for an X-ray machine — and one arrived at Aklavik's All Saints Hospital within a few months. Hersey recovered from his wounds and retired from the Canadian army in 1954. By the time Inspector Eames retired in 1946, he had been promoted to Assistant Commissioner of the RCMP.

Bibliography

Anderson, F.W., and Art Downs. *The Death of Albert Johnson.* Surrey: Heritage House Publishing Company Ltd., 2000.

Dobrowolsky, Helene. *Law of the Yukon: A Pictorial History of the Mounted Police in the Yukon.* Whitehorse: Lost Moose, the Yukon Publishers, 1995.

North, Dick. *The Mad Trapper of Rat River.* Toronto: Macmillan of Canada, 1972.

North, Dick. *Trackdown: the search for the mad trapper.* Toronto: Macmillan of Canada, 1989.

Reid, Sheila. *Wings of a Hero.* St. Catharines: Vanwell Publishing Ltd., 1997.

Saul, Donovan T. (editor). *Red Serge and Stetsons.* Victoria: Horsdal & Schubart, 1993.

Acknowledgments

Putting together a book is the result of teamwork. Sandra Phinney encouraged me to approach Kara Turner, associate publisher at Altitude Publishing. Marvin Zivitz dug up newspaper articles to get me started. The staff at McGill University's library, as well as the Yukon, Northwest Territories, and National Archives, helped me find articles and documents about the manhunt.

Nicole Smith from the RCMP's Historical Office, and Celeste Rider from the Saskatchewan Genealogical Society, sent me information about the members who participated in the manhunt. David Kyllo, from the Historical Society of Hudson's Hope, B.C., kindly shared an interview that his parents had conducted with trapper Noel Verville.

Sharon Garon and Bernie Schmachtel provided a quiet place at their home in Hay River, where I wrote an early draft of the book. One of their cats, Tonka, would often perch on my shoulder to watch as I crafted sentences. My editor, Jill Foran, was a treat to work with as she gently proposed ways to improve the story.

My sister, Catherine, who has been watching over me since I was born, read the manuscript and provided valuable suggestions to improve the text. She was excited about this

Acknowledgments

project from the outset and reassured me that I was on the right track.

Marian Scott mentored me when I first became a journalist and encouraged me to keep writing. Last but certainly not least, I'd like to thank my parents, Jeannette and Selim, for being proud that I write.

About the Author

Hélèna Katz is an award-winning Montreal journalist whose work has appeared in magazines and newspapers in Canada and the United States. She earned a Bachelor of Arts degree in psychology from McGill University and is currently completing a Masters degree in criminology at the Université de Montréal. This is her first book.

Photo Credits

KLONDIKE JOE BOYLE
The Globetrotting Adventures of a Fearless Canadian Spy

"...man with the heart of a Viking
and the simple faith of a child."
Joe Boyle epitaph

An adventurer and a natural leader, Joe Whiteside Boyle blazed the White Pass to the Yukon and was among the few who scratched a fortune from the Klondike. During World War I, he was a spymaster working behind Russian lines. He cheated death many times to become the "Saviour of Rumania," and in the process fell in love with a queen.

 True stories. Truly Canadian.

ISBN 1-55153-969-1

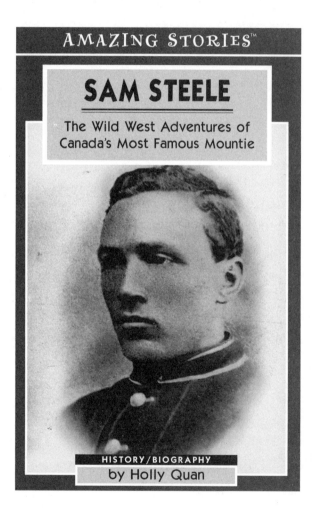

AMAZING STORIES™

SAM STEELE

The Wild West Adventures of
Canada's Most Famous Mountie

HISTORY/BIOGRAPHY
by Holly Quan

SAM STEELE

The Wild West Adventures of Canada's Most Famous Mountie

"…Now I had the Great Lone Land before me where it is a man's own fault if he fails while he has health and strength."
Sam Steele

Once or twice in our lives, some of us are lucky enough to witness or even to participate in an event of historical importance. Sam Steele made a career of it. During the pioneering years of the Canadian West, Sam Steele was not only present but took an active role in virtually every significant historical event. Sam Steele was an adventurer and a heroic figure who commanded awe and respect. He just did the right thing. At the right time. In the right place.

True stories. Truly Canadian.

ISBN 1-55153-997-7

ROBERT SERVICE
A Great Canadian Poet's Romance with the North

"It was Saturday night, and from the various bars I heard sounds of revelry. The line popped into my mind: 'A bunch of boys were whooping it up' and it stuck there. Good enough for a start."
Robert Service

Robert William Service lived a life of adventure. Best known for his world-famous poems such as the *Shooting of Dan McGrew,* he drew much of his inspiration from the great Canadian North. Despite his many adventures in Europe and around the world, the Yukon remained a strong influence on the poet until his death in 1958.

True stories. Truly Canadian.

ISBN 1-55153-956-X

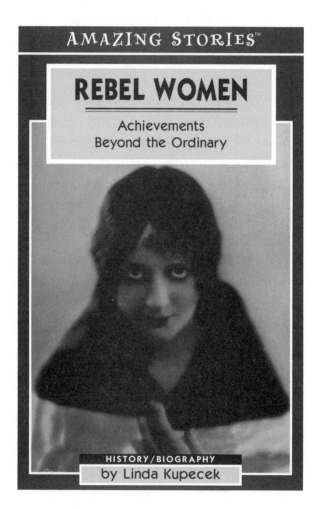

REBEL WOMEN
Achievements
Beyond the Ordinary

*"It seems to me there is always somebody
to tell you [you] can't accomplish a thing, and
to discourage you from even attempting it. If you
are going to let other people decide what
you are able to do, I don't think you
will ever do much of anything."*
Katherine Stinson

Many famous women of the west are celebrated elsewhere. In this book, we meet lesser known rebels, those who lived with passion, individuality, and courage. These are women who dared to follow their own path through life; women who dared to be different.

True stories. Truly Canadian.

ISBN 1-55153-991-8